6|08-11x   12/11- 12ₓ   R

gc 5 //8-/3ₓ

ON THE ROAD

Kerouac's Ragged American Journey

TWAYNE'S MASTERWORK STUDIES

Robert Lecker, General Editor

ON THE ROAD

Kerouac's Ragged American Journey

Robert Holton
Okanagan University College

TWAYNE PUBLISHERS
New York

Twayne's Masterwork Studies No. 172

On the Road: Kerouac's Ragged American Journey
Robert Holton

Copyright © 1999 by Twayne Publishers

Twayne Publishers
1633 Broadway
New York, NY 10019

Library of Congress Cataloging-in-Publication Data
Holton, Robert, 1950–
        On the road : Kerouac's ragged American journey / Robert
Holton.
        p. cm. — (Twayne's masterwork studies ; no. 172)
        Includes bibliographical references and index.
        ISBN 0-8057-1692-0 (alk. paper)
        1. Kerouac, Jack, 1922–1969. On the road. 2. Autobiographical
fiction, American—History and criticism. 3. Beat generation in
literature. I. Title. II. Series.
        PS3521.E735 O533   1999
        813'.54—dc21
                                                    99-33122
                                                    CIP

This paper meets the requirements of ANSI/NISO Z3948-1992 (Permanence of Paper).

10 9 8 7 6 5 4 3 2 1

Printed in the United States of America

For Daniel and Jake

Jack Kerouac in 1956.
Photograph courtesy of Walter Lehrman.

Contents

Note on the References and Acknowledgments   ix

Chronology: Jack Kerouac's Life and Works   xi

LITERARY AND HISTORICAL CONTEXT
   1.   Historical Background   3
   2.   The Importance of *On the Road*   7
   3.   Critical Reception   11

A READING
   4.   Setting Out   19
   5.   The First Journey   38
   6.   The Second Journey   67
   7.   The Third Journey   89
   8.   The Final Journey   112

Notes and References   125

Selected Bibliography   129

Index   133

Note on the References and Acknowledgments

All quotations from *On the Road* are taken from the Penguin paperback edition (1976), the most widely available edition of the novel. The 1991 edition also includes Ann Charters's insightful introduction. Quotations from Kerouac's letters are taken from *Selected Letters, 1940–1956*, edited by Ann Charters (1995).

Portions of this study appeared in an earlier version in *Modern Fiction Studies* 41, no. 2 (Summer 1995).

My thanks to Walter Lehrman for permission to use his photograph of Kerouac and to the Allen Ginsberg Estate for helping me to track it down.

Work on this book was supported by Social Sciences and Humanities Research Council of Canada and by Okanagan University College Grants in Aid of Research.

I would like to express my thanks to Lee Simons and Natasha Tusikov, who assisted with research during this project and Gordon Ball who provided timely advice. I would also like to thank the many students who have read and discussed *On the Road* in my American literature classes. Finally, I would like to thank Ken Snyder for introducing me to American literature.

Chronology: Jack Kerouac's Life and Works

1922	Jean Louis (Jack) Kerouac born 12 March 1922 in Lowell, Massachusetts, the third and last child of Joseph Alcide Léon (Leo) Kirouack (a printer) and Gabrielle Lévesque (a shoe factory worker). Both parents were born in Quebec and immigrated to this increasingly industrialized area. The two older Kerouac children are Gerard (b. 1916) and Caroline, called Nin (b. 1918).
1923	Leo Kerouac opens his own print shop. Business does well enough to allow the family several moves to progressively larger houses in "better" neighborhoods.
1926	In July, Gerard, Jack's "saintly" older brother, dies from rheumatic fever. Leo's drinking and gambling intensifies as does the fighting between the Kerouac parents.
1928	Jack starts school, still speaking only French.
1933	The school librarian forms "The Scribbler's Club," which Jack attends with his friend Sebastian (Sammy) Sampas. First short story called "The Cop on the Beat." Begins a lifelong habit of carrying a pocket notebook and writing down short character sketches and other observations as they occur to him. Leo's business in decline.
1936	Merrimack River floods its banks, damaging Leo's uninsured printing business, which is placed in receivership.
1937	Caroline Kerouac leaves home to marry against her parents' wishes. Jack stars in Lowell's football victory over neighboring high school.
1938	Jack becomes reacquainted with Sebastian Sampas, whose idealism and literary interests bring them close. Meets Mary Carney, later fictionalized as Maggie Cassidy. Leo's chronic financial problems result in the loss of his printing business. Jack scores an important touchdown in the Thanksgiving football game, bringing him to the attention of football scouts.

1939	High school graduation. Offered football scholarships at both Boston College and Columbia. Encouraged by his mother, he chooses Columbia, despite having to attend qualifying year at Horace Mann prep school in the Bronx, where he excels athletically and academically. Publishes "The Brother," in the *Horace Mann Quarterly*. Meets Henri Cru (Remi Boncoeur in *On the Road*) and Seymour Wyse. Discovers Harlem jazz clubs. World War II breaks out in September.
1940	Publishes "Une Veille de Noel" in the *Quarterly*. Finishes at Horace Mann and returns to Lowell, spending time with Sebastian Sampas. Starts at Columbia and suffers a broken leg during a football game in October. Spends much of his winter reading, immersing himself in Thomas Wolfe's writing.
1941	Disenchanted with Columbia and football. Quits and returns to Lowell, where he works a series of jobs, including a stint as a sports reporter for the *Lowell Sun*. In December, Pearl Harbor is bombed.
1942	Reads Dostoyevsky extensively. Leaves for Washington, D.C., where he works various jobs before returning to Massachusetts. Ships out as a dishwasher on the merchant ship SS *Dorchester*. Works on *The Sea Is My Brother*. Returns to Columbia but has a falling-out with football coach and returns to Lowell. In New York, he meets Edie Parker, who later becomes his first wife.
1943	Joins the Navy in February but unable to adjust to military discipline. Confined to a psychiatric ward until May, when he is discharged. Meets fellow-patient, William Holmes Hubbard, or "Big Slim," who offers to introduce him to Mississippi Gene—both mentioned in *On the Road*. Ships out in June aboard another merchant ship, the SS *George Weems*, bound for Liverpool carrying bombs. Returns to New York in October and spends time at the 115th Street apartment shared by Edie Parker and Joan Vollmer Adams.
1944	Death of Sammy Sampas. Meets Lucien Carr, Allan Ginsberg, and William Burroughs. Becomes involved in Carr's killing of David Kammerer and is arrested as a material witness. Marries Edie on 22 August, partly in order to get bail money. 115th Street apartment becomes the hub of the emerging Beat scene.
1945	Begins work on *The Town and the City*. Works with Burroughs on *And the Hippos Were Boiled in Their Tanks,* based on the Carr/Kammerer case. Hospitalized in December for thrombophlebitis resulting from excessive Benzedrine use. Leo Kerouac is diagnosed with cancer of the spleen.

Chronology

1946	Leo Kerouac dies. William Burroughs and Joan Vollmer (Old Bull Lee and Jane Lee in *On the Road*) move to Texas. Lucien Carr released from jail. Jack's marriage to Edie Parker annulled. In December, Jack meets Neal Cassady and LuAnne Henderson (Dean Moriarty and Marylou in *On the Road*).
1947	In July, begins the first trip that becomes part of *On the Road*. In October, returns to New York and his writing.
1948	Meets John Clellon Holmes and coins the term "Beat Generation." Completes *The Town and the City*. Writes a draft of *On the Road*. On 29 December, Cassady, with LuAnne, and Al Hinckle arrive at Nin's home in North Carolina where Jack and Mémère (his mother) are visiting, thus beginning the second trip described in *On the Road*.
1949	Returns to New York in February. In March, *The Town and the City* is accepted for publication. Moves to Denver with his mother in the spring, returning within a few months. In August, Neal and Jack begin *On the Road*'s third trip.
1950	*The Town and the City* is published to lukewarm reviews. Continues work on *On the Road*. Leaves for Mexico City in June with Neal, *On the Road*'s fourth and last trip. Returns to New York and writing in the fall. Meets Joan Haverty, who becomes his second wife on 17 November.
1951	Neal's "Joan Anderson" letter inspires Jack's spontaneous bop prose, and he writes new version of *On the Road* on a single roll of paper in three weeks. Reads manuscripts of Burroughs's *Junkie* and Holmes's *Go*. Separates from Joan Haverty, who is pregnant. Denies paternity. Hospitalized with thrombophlebitis in the fall, then leaves to visit Neal and Carolyn Cassady in San Francisco where he works on *Visions of Cody*.
1952	Lives with Cassadys until April and (with Neal's encouragement) has an affair with Carolyn. Works on *Visions of Cody*. On 16 February, Jan Kerouac is born to his estranged wife Joan. Holmes's *Go* is accepted for publication. Works on *Doctor Sax* in Mexico while staying with Burroughs. Travels extensively while writing "The Railroad Earth" and, by the end of the year, is back with his mother in New York.
1953	Travels west. Works on railroad and ships out on SS *William Carruth*. Writes *Maggie Cassidy* based on relationship with Mary Carney. Relationship with Alene Lee leads to the writing of *The Subterraneans* in 72 hours. Works on "Essentials of Spontaneous Prose."
1954	Stays with Cassadys in California. Begins serious study of Buddhism. A mystical experience in a Lowell church reveals the

relationship of Beat and beatific. Works on *San Francisco Blues* and *Some of the Dharma*.

1955   Publication of "Jazz of the Beat Generation" and acceptance for publication of "The Mexican Girl" and "cityCityCITY." Works on *Mexico City Blues* and *Tristessa* in Mexico. In San Francisco for the now-legendary Six Gallery reading when Ginsberg first performs "Howl."

1956   Visits North Carolina and works on *Visions of Gerard*. Travels to California and works on *The Scripture of the Golden Eternity* and "Old Angel Midnight." Spends nine weeks as fire lookout in Washington, described in *Desolation Angels*. Finishes *Tristessa* in Mexico City.

1957   Works with Burroughs on *Naked Lunch* in Tangier. Travels in Europe. Relationship with Joyce Johnson. *On the Road* is published to a rave *New York Times* review, making Kerouac instantly famous. Works on *The Dharma Bums* in Florida.

1958   Publication of *The Subterraneans* and *The Dharma Bums*. Moves to Long Island. Begins work on *Lonesome Traveler*. Marijuana charge leads to five-year sentence for Neal Cassady.

1959   Works with Robert Frank and others on *Pull My Daisy*. Publication of *Doctor Sax, Mexico City Blues,* and *Maggie Cassidy*. Travels to California and appears on *The Steve Allen Show*.

1960   Visits California and experiences a breakdown in Big Sur, the result of chronic alcoholism. Publication of *Tristessa, The Scripture of the Golden Eternity,* and *Lonesome Traveler*.

1961   Publication of *Book of Dreams* and *Pull My Daisy*. Moves to Florida. Travels to Mexico. Works on *Desolation Angels* and *Big Sur*.

1962   Returns to Long Island. Publication of *Big Sur*.

1963   Publication of *Visions of Gerard*. Cassady visits from California.

1964   Returns to Florida. Meets Cassady with Ken Kesey and the Merry Pranksters. Death of sister Caroline.

1965   Trip to France leads to writing of *Satori in Paris*. Works on *Pic*. Publication of *Desolation Angels*.

1966   Publication of *Satori in Paris*. Moves to Hyannis, then Lowell. Marriage to third wife, Stella Sampas, sister of close childhood friend and intellectual influence Sebastian Sampas.

1967   Works on *Vanity of Duluoz*.

1968   Publication of *Vanity of Duluoz*. Death of Neal Cassady on railroad tracks in Mexico. Guest appearance on William F. Buckley's TV show *Firing Line*. Returns to Florida.

1969   Suffers abdominal hemorrhage on 20 October and dies the next day. Death caused by chronic alcoholism.

Chronology

1971   Publication of *Scattered Poems* and *Pic*.
1972   Publication of *Visions of Cody*.
1977   Publication of *Heaven and Other Poems*.
1992   Publication of *Pomes All Sizes*.
1993   Publication of *Old Angel Midnight* and *Good Blonde and Others*.
1995   Publication of *Book of Blues* and *Selected Letters, 1940–1956* (ed. Ann Charters).
1997   Publication of *Some of the Dharma*.

LITERARY AND
HISTORICAL CONTEXT

1

Historical Background

In considering Jack Kerouac's *On the Road*, it is important to consider as well the historical period in which it was produced. This is true of any work of art of course, yet it seems particularly crucial for this novel, responding as it does so directly to a specific and unique postwar moment in American history, a moment that allowed the Beat Generation to come into being and to flourish briefly before conditions changed and other social formations emerged. Like the roman candles Kerouac compares it to early in *On the Road*, the original Beat movement was short-lived, yet it has left a lasting impression. The travels on which this novel is based took place in the late 1940s and very early 1950s. Although it was not finally published until 1957, most of the writing was completed much earlier, while the postwar sensibility was beginning to take shape. Sometimes the subject of ridicule, sometimes the subject of adulation, by the late 1950s the Beats—and Kerouac in particular—had seized the imagination of postwar America more powerfully than any other comparable movement. And the publication of *On the Road* was a central event in this phenomenon.

With the close of World War II, America emerged as a dominant force in global politics and economics. Ordinary Americans entered a period of prosperity and optimism that showed no imminent signs of abating. Progress appeared possible on many fronts, and new technologies promised to make life easier at home and in the workplace. Education held out the promise of unprecedented class mobility, as veterans returning from the war benefited from the GI Bill's provision of access to postsecondary education. As a result, more students than ever crowded the classes of American universities. Traditional religions were in decline, and the search for meaning and identity created bestsellers out of *The Power of Positive Thinking* and *How to Win Friends and Influence People*. The mass media were expanding into new areas, and television in particular pointed to a new kind of American culture. With the increasing levels of disposable income came the emergence of a youth culture with its own heroes, its own taste in music, movies, clothes, even food. This era was the time of the birth of McDonald's restaurant, the forerunner of the massive retail franchises that would revolutionize (and standardize) American consumption. The fact that more Americans were driving than ever before not only boosted the economy but also created the mobility that allowed people to move out of the cities and into the new suburbs and permitted the development of the modern shopping mall.

This mobility provides a useful example of change in the traditional fabric of American life with direct relevance to Kerouac's *On the Road*. In 1956, the Federal-Aid Highway Act was passed, leading to the construction of the new controlled-access interstate highways that would soon cover the United States. On one hand, the new highway system was obviously progressive: providing a safer means of transportation, it also increased speed limits and improved traveling times. But it is important to remember that an important aspect of an older America was being lost in this modernization. No longer would America's highways lead travelers into and through the lives and towns of the nation. The new system moved traffic outside populated areas and insulated local life from travelers. The great journeys across Route 66—enshrined in Steinbeck's *The Grapes of Wrath*, in the pop music classic "Get Your Kicks on Route 66," and on television's *Route 66*—would never be the same, as America's most famous highway was becoming a matter of historical record rather than contemporary culture. Within a few years, traffic had shifted to more efficient but less intimate routes, enabling a more homogeneous and less idiosyncratic traveling experience. Indeed, the voyages of Sal Paradise and Dean Moriarty depend in part for their resonance on the America that these smaller highways led them through.

Balancing the general mood of optimism and prosperity, however, was another legacy of war. World War II's hostilities had not simply concluded but shifted to a new site of conflict as former allies became locked in a Cold War tension heightened by the threat of the new military technology, devastating beyond comprehension: the Bomb. It became clear that the next war, which appeared to be a real and imminent possibility, might not be a matter of winners and losers but instead could bring about mutual annihilation—"the end of civilization as we know it," to use a common phrase. Fear of the enemy, internal and external, led to the remarkable suppression of dissent known as McCarthyism. Citizens who held—or were suspected of holding—"subversive" views were persecuted in a variety of ways, and the height of this crackdown came in the 1953 execution of Julius and Ethel Rosenberg, alleged to have passed American nuclear secrets to the Soviets. In considering Kerouac's scathing use of terms such as "cop-souls" or the "American Gestapo," it is important to remember the political climate of the times.

The other side of this attempt to eradicate dissent was a corresponding emphasis on normality, on conformism and standardization. As early as David Riesman's *The Lonely Crowd* in 1950, studies began to pour forth on the subject of conformism, concerned with the degree to which the homogenization of America was well under way: *The Organization Man, The Man in the Grey Flannel Suit, Beyond Conformity, Growing Up Absurd,* and many others. Orwell's *1984* and Huxley's *Brave New World* were studied closely as indications of what might lie in store. A degree of conformity is essential to social cohesion of course, but it seemed to many analysts, from academic social psychologists to magazine writers, that the excessive conformism of the postwar period had the potential to eliminate the individual spirit that, they felt, had made America a great nation.

Kerouac looked back with nostalgia to an earlier time, sometimes his own prewar childhood in Lowell, Massachusetts, and some-

times even further, to a lost America—really an imaginary America—
that offered a sense of contemporary possibility. In "The Origins of
the Beat Generation," he praises the America of the past: "Like my
grandfather this America was invested with wild selfbelieving individuality and this had begun to disappear around the end of World War
II."[1] This spirit has been replaced with "a sinister new kind of effi-
ciency," he maintains, which is less and less tolerant of those who do
not fit in to the dominant patterns.[2] "Take another look at me," he
writes in *Desolation Angels*:

> people are scared to look at me because I really look like an
> escaped mental patient with enough physical strength and innate
> dog-sense to manage outside an institution to feed myself and go
> from place to place in a world growing gradually narrower in its
> views about eccentricity every day.... [I was] more fit for the
> Holy Russia of [Dostoyevsky's] 19th Century than for this mod-
> ern America of crew cuts and sullen faces in Pontiacs.[3]

For Kerouac, it is precisely with these misfits and eccentrics that hope
lies: "suddenly," he writes, this spirit "began to emerge again, the hipsters began to appear gliding around saying 'Crazy, man' "("Origins,"
59).

Kerouac searched in those areas of the social world that
appeared less able or less likely to embrace (or be embraced by)
modernity and its streamlined processes, for people less likely to
appear as consumers or laborers in franchised freeway restaurants:
hoboes and drug addicts, the "perverted" and the insane, the visionaries and the artists. In African American jazz culture, for example, segregated as it was in pre-Civil Rights era America, Kerouac found a
model of a culture flourishing in its separation from the mainstream,
indeed flourishing partly because of its separation from a mainstream
that had the power to destroy real art and culture. Despite its deliberate sense of hip, postwar newness, of contemporaneity, *On the Road*
remains, to a remarkable degree, a requiem for an America that Kerouac felt was vanishing faster than he could record it.

2

The Importance of *On the Road*

Very few literary works have the kind of impact that *On the Road* had on the culture of its time. And judging by Jack Kerouac's fate, perhaps that is just as well. On the strength of Gilbert Millstein's review in the *New York Times*, Kerouac was swept up into what is now described as a media feeding frenzy. The general public had been gaining awareness of a new subcultural phenomenon—through publicity generated by the "Howl" obscenity trial, for example, which was occurring that same summer. With the appearance of *On the Road*, the media thought they had the perfect representative of this strange new Beat culture, another in the line of American angry and alienated young men such as those portrayed by Marlon Brando and James Dean. Kerouac was handsome and articulate, athletic and vulnerable, and the fact that he was a real person rather than a character in a movie, a serious writer rather than a Hollywood actor, did not stand in the way. Offers soon came from television interview shows and mass-market magazines such as *Mademoiselle* and *Life, Playboy* and *Esquire*. He was hired to do readings in nightclubs and on television. The possibility of a film version starring Marlon Brando was discussed, and Hollywood offered more than $100,000 for the screen rights—a large sum at the time—but Kerouac's agent held out for more.

The publication of *On the Road* marked a turning point in postwar American cultural history. In the era of Cold War conformism, it helped to define a space of radical dissent that nevertheless avoided the pitfalls of political partisanship. For many, it provided a sense of an alternative lifestyle, the reinvention of bohemian culture for a new generation. Since the original Parisian Bohemians of postrevolutionary France, talented and imaginative people have often turned to one or another form of bohemian existence to compensate for the limitations of conventional ways of life, and at this moment it seemed there was an enormous desire for such an alternative. As William Burroughs observed, "After 1957 *On the Road* sold a trillion levis and a million espresso machines, and also sent countless kids on the road."[1] Unfortunately for Kerouac, however, his book had appeared just as America became hungry for a new fad, and the whole phenomenon—literary and social—was soon consigned to that level. As the "beatnik" craze exploded, Kerouac was caught in the middle, unable to prevent his ideas from becoming devalued and commercialized. He was intense and fiercely dedicated to his work, yet before long Kerouac and the Beat Generation were fodder for *Mad* magazine parodies. America's best-known "beatnik" was Maynard G. Krebs, a television sitcom character on *The Many Loves of Dobie Gillis* played by Bob Denver, who would later establish himself as Gilligan on *Gilligan's Island*. Popular films and novels thrive on sensationalistic representations of sex and violence, and the entertainment industry soon seized on the "beatnik" image and exploited it. Kerouac even lost the rights to the title *The Beat Generation* when Hollywood produced a movie by that name about a villainous rapist.

One commentator who continued to take it all seriously was FBI chief J. Edgar Hoover, who declared that the three greatest menaces to America were "Communists, Beatniks, [and] Eggheads."[2] Hoover's response is interesting, and it leads into the question of the novel's political impact. If Hoover found this culture dangerously radical, many others, hoping to locate a political agenda somewhere in this rebellion, found it disappointingly conservative, lacking focus, even nihilistic. From Norman Podhoretz, who compared Kerouac's description of "happy, ecstatic" African American life to the rationales of southern plantation owners, to Simon Frith who described his attitude as "weirdly racist," readers have questioned his racial understanding.[3] Despite frequent criticism of the attitudes toward race that the book articulates, it is interesting to note the response of Eldridge Cleaver, noted Black Panther activist and author of *Soul on Ice*. Citing Kerouac's lyrical description of Denver's "colored section," Cleaver recognized in the Beats the first step in a longer process of social disaffiliation that he believed could ultimately ally alienated whites with African Americans in a resistance to the American power structure. This analysis finds political potential at a deeper cultural level, linking Kerouac's imaginary (cultural) racial identification with the sense of political identification that finally drew white Civil Rights protesters to join blacks in opposition to the systemic racism of the period.[4]

As the Beat movement gradually evolved into the hippies and yippies of another decade, *On the Road* remained a key text in the attempt to define an identity outside the mainstream. While Kerouac's own opinions in the 1960s shifted toward intolerance and even bigotry, his novel was swept along in a cultural tidal wave he could not hope to control. Tom Hayden, later to become one of America's most influential student radicals, describes the liberating effect of *On the Road*: "Kerouac aroused a deep desire 'to prowl in the wilderness' among young readers like myself."[5] Kerouac's influence on contemporary popular culture is even stronger. Bob Dylan, for example, recalls that it "was Ginsberg and Jack Kerouac who inspired me first."[6] And in England, like many others, John Lennon was an avid reader of Kerouac's work while he was a student.[7] *On the Road* did not cause the enormous turmoil of the Beat Generation or the 1960s movements that followed it, but it was certainly one of the important catalysts.

While the novel was invisible on most English department reading lists, it was nonetheless widely read and discussed on campuses all across America. As Sven Birkerts notes, it was an integral part of the "non-curricular education" of the time.[8] Thomas Pynchon, who describes himself "post-Beat," considers *On the Road* "one of the greatest American novels." In the introduction to *Slow Learner*, he refers to Kerouac's novel as one of the "centrifugal lures" drawing young writers and others to investigate the "expansion of possibilities" that was occurring.[9] Kerouac's literary legacy is to be found less in the specifics of his spontaneous prose model than in his openness to a range of experience—personal and social—previously ignored. And his willingness to violate literary convention—even the conventions of modernism—in order to express the intensity and immediacy of his perceptions continues to offer an example. Jazz drummer Max Roach once commented that Bop originated when musicians "kept reading about rockets and jets and radar, and you can't play 4/4 music in times like that" (McNally, 82). *On the Road* provided no precise blueprint for later art, but it did make an important contribution to an awareness that literature too had to adapt "in times like that."

In his 1989 re-reading for *Harper's,* Birkerts expressed his disappointment in *On the Road,* but admitted that he was not so much reading Kerouac's text "as taking stock—of those times, of these times, of myself in both"(315). While older readers who return to *On the Road* in search of lost youth may be disappointed, new readers continue to turn to it. Sales of the novel are strong again, a fortieth anniversary hardcover edition has been released, new biographies are being produced, and many recordings of Kerouac's work are now available. Signs of Kerouac's influence are ubiquitous still. A 40-year-old photograph of Kerouac outside a bar at the time of *On the Road*'s publication has recently been used in one trendy clothes ad, and his name is dropped conspicuously in another. Kerouac memorabilia fetches high prices. Rumors of a major Hollywood film are circulating once again.

3

Critical Reception

The critical reception of *On the Road* has been marked by astonishing extremes, extremes that can be seen even in the earliest reviews that greeted it. As luck would have it, Orville Prescott, the regular book reviewer for the influential *New York Times,* was vacationing when Kerouac's novel first appeared. While Prescott, a man of more conservative tastes, would not likely have reacted well to Kerouac's picaresque narrative, it was given instead to Gilbert Millstein, a reviewer who had long had an interest in the Beat writers and had previously helped Kerouac's friend John Clellon Holmes to publish his "This Is the Beat Generation" in the *New York Times Magazine.* Upon publication then, *On the Road*'s initial review in America's most important arbiter of literary taste ensured the book's success: "a major novel" wrote Gilbert Millstein, "an authentic work of art" whose appearance is a "historic occasion." The writing, he declared, displays at times "a beauty almost breathtaking."[1] His publisher, Viking, sent the chronically impoverished Kerouac a case of champagne that morning.

While Millstein's lavish praise for Kerouac's book established his position as a writer to be reckoned with, most of the early reviews were more negative—at times even outright hostile. A few days later, another review—this one in the *Times'* Sunday edition—took a very different position. While "readable and entertaining," *On the Road* seemed to David Dempsey little more than a "sideshow": "the freaks" may be "fascinating," he observed, but "they are hardly part of our lives." That Kerouac's narrative could maintain "a morally neutral point of view" while recounting incidents of blatant immorality seemed to this reviewer unacceptable.[2] This opinion was shared by Herbert Gold, whose review in *The Nation* argued that it was a "proof of illness rather than a creation of art."[3] Not surprisingly, the review published in the more radical *Village Voice* was positive, acknowledging the book as "a rallying point for the elusive spirit of rebellion of these times."[4] In all, the reviews were mixed at best, but the book climbed the best-seller lists quickly on the strength of the initial *Times* review and the controversy that ensued.

For a time Kerouac was the subject of enormous attention. As Holmes put it, people expected him to be the "new, young Marlon Brando of literature," and these expectations were simply too much.[5] After so many years of working in obscurity, of buoying himself against rejections by publishers, Kerouac was extremely vulnerable to fame once it came his way. He was very well-read, and he considered his work to have serious literary merit. When the literary establishment treated him and his writing as a cultural novelty item, and a distasteful one at that, he was deeply wounded. Publication of his subsequent writing did nothing to change critical opinion; if anything it made things worse. Typical of the response is Truman Capote's quip that Kerouac's work "isn't writing at all—it's typing."[6] This sort of ridicule was devastating to a writer whose dedication was beyond question and whose willingness to experiment with literary form and convention left him open to the uncomprehending responses of unsympathetic critics. Certainly, Kerouac's writing can be extremely uneven, but it became critically fashionable to place Kerouac's work in that category of the useless but not quite forgettable that includes yo-yos, hula hoops, and ducktail haircuts.

The notoriety of Kerouac and his central position in the Beat phenomenon that erupted—due in large part to the publication of *On the Road*—ensured that the novel would not be forgotten. Kerouac has received a great deal of attention in recent decades, but the majority involves the man rather than his work. Biographical studies have proliferated, as have studies of the Beat Generation, but critical commentary has not been so abundant. In the years following its publication, *On the Road* seemed not to fit into any traditional generic category and was thus deemed to be a deeply flawed work. While a deeply flawed man may retain the interest of readers, a deeply flawed work tends not to retain the interest of critics. Despite their critical insights, important studies by George Dardess, Tim Hunt, John Tytell, and Regina Weinreich that argued for the literary strengths of Kerouac's writing had little effect on the reigning attitudes to Kerouac's work. Graduate students were advised against working on it and in some cases, the strictures against studying Kerouac's work were sufficient to relegate critics who embarked on it to a marginality of their own. In 1973, for example, Carole Vopat noted that "Nothing has been published about Jack Kerouac for seven years."[7]

A trickle of studies did continue however; these tended to focus on traditional approaches to the novel's quest motif, mythic patterns, and religious impulse, and many continued their negative appraisal. Melvin Askew, for example, before exploring Kerouac's relation to American quest mythology, makes clear that he is doing so in spite of the "painfully evident" fact of the novel's "failure of artistic realization." Two long introductory paragraphs characterize it as "treacherous" and "tedious," "neither exciting, illuminating, or enduring." It is, in one way or another, "shabby" and "frightening," and Askew questions whether it should even be discussed in serious journals.[8] A decade later, Vopat was willing to give Kerouac a little more credence. While accepting that Askew might have been right in his estimation that Kerouac "leaves a smirch on . . . classic American literature," she is not quite so damning: he "is a not a great writer, but he is a good writer, and has more depth and control than his critics allow." Contrary to many readers, Vopat maintains that Kerouac's achievement is to have provided a portrait of characters who "take to the road not to find life but to leave it all behind." For her, "life" consists of those categories such as maturity, responsibility, and purposeful decision-making that, she argues, Sal and Dean "flee" in order to avoid "self-analysis, self-awareness, thinking" (303).

Later on, as political concerns such as race and gender became increasingly important in critical evaluation, *On the Road* was considered by many to be hopelessly conservative, strangely naive, and senselessly self-destructive. Ellen Friedman, for example, suggests that *On the Road* does more to strengthen than to challenge the master narratives that legitimate the gendered hierarchies of an unjust social structure.[9] And Dick Hebdige dismisses the "breathless panegyrics of Jack Kerouac (who carried the idealization of Negro culture to almost ludicrous extremes)."[10] Critics over the decades and across a variety of critical approaches have typically been unable to find a way to deal with *On the Road,* and the result has been the relegation of the novel to a critical ghetto. It is obvious that *On the Road* will not help sort out correct solutions to the dilemmas of gender and race that continue to afflict America. Kerouac was himself extremely conflicted on these issues and capable of outrageous sexism and racism. If we go to *On the Road* looking for a novel that will fit comfortably with the literary canon, we will be disappointed. If we go to it looking for models of coherent subjectivity and responsible citizenship, we will be bewildered. If we go to it looking for clean and idealistic solutions to the social problems of the 1990s, we will be appalled. Yet *On the Road* is one of the key texts that shaped American culture in the decades after the war, and if we go to it to understand that relation, our reading may be rewarded.

Ragged is one of the most frequently repeated words in the novel, and Kerouac presented the ragged America that he experienced in a prose conveying the immediacy of that experience. This ragged quality leaves the novel filled with unresolved tensions, blatant contradictions, and distressing perplexities rather than providing the orderly and well-polished surfaces of High Art. A sentence in *On the Road* suggests this dichotomy between traditional art and his ragged chronicle of life.

> Dean had come to my house, slept several nights there, waiting
> for me; spent afternoons talking to my aunt as she worked on a

great rag rug woven of all the clothes in my family for years, which was now finished and spread on my bedroom floor, as complex and rich as the passage of time itself; and then he had left, two days before I had arrived, crossing my path probably somewhere in Pennsylvania or Ohio, to go to San Francisco. (107)

The strands of Sal's life appear too unruly to be woven into any finished work, and Kerouac's "great rag rug" was never really completed, nor could it be. He continued to revise and rewrite throughout his short life.

It is possible that in today's postdeconstructionist critical climate—more welcoming to works that call into question the line between High Art and low art, canonical and noncanonical, more able to consider works that raise more questions than they answer—*On the Road* may finally attract more interesting critical commentary. Kerouac has been cited as a forerunner to the sort of poststructuralism discussed by Gilles Deleuze and Felix Guattari in *Anti-Oedipus,* for example, and more theoretically informed critical approaches will no doubt begin to yield interesting results. In 1983, Tim Hunt, one of the best of Kerouac's critics, looked forward to the time "when Kerouac finally acquires readers to replace his fans."[11] Years later, he was still waiting. In the recent introduction to his reissued study, *Kerouac's Crooked Road,* he points to some promising directions: "A postmodern Kerouac? A postcolonial Kerouac? A Kerouac whose life and work might bear on our current concerns with ethnicity and class? These are positions waiting to be constructed."[12]

A READING

4

Setting Out

Jack Kerouac's *On the Road* begins with the word *I*. On one level, the use of a first-person narrator is most easily explained by the fact that the book was written—at least in part—in answer to Joan Haverty Kerouac's question to her husband Jack: "What did you and Neal really do?"[1] The book may be read, then, as a thinly veiled autobiography, and the reader may trace the characters and events back to their originals. From a more literary point of view, the first-person narrator connects this novel to American classics such as Melville's *Moby Dick* and Twain's *The Adventures of Huckleberry Finn,* which examine, among other things, the possibilities of escape from American middle-class propriety. Leslie Fiedler considered this "flight of the dreamer from the drab duties of home and town" a fundamental narrative pattern in American culture.[2] And in the twentieth century, F. Scott Fitzgerald's *The Great Gatsby* and J. D. Salinger's *The Catcher in the Rye*—to mention only two well-known examples—recount the explorations of first-person male narrators finding their way in the world.

Yet it is also the case that both of the other major works of Beat literature, Allen Ginsberg's "Howl" and William Burroughs's *Naked Lunch,* begin with the word *I*, a coincidence that not only suggests the intensely personal nature of much Beat writing but also points to a preoccupation with the nature of the self, its integrity and coherence in light of the new pressures of the postwar period. One of the most important concerns of *On the Road* is Sal's struggle to establish or invent a stable identity even as all stable structures are being undermined and self-knowledge proves elusive. The recurrent shifts and collapses of identity he experiences in the course of the novel place the *I* that begins the book in question by the end.

As in any first-person narrative, there are at least three layers of narrativity to disentangle, although in *On the Road* these are not always clearly distinguishable. At the most obvious level, we have Sal Paradise the character, whose adventures are detailed in the narrative. One level above, we have Sal Paradise the narrator, detailing the events with the benefit of a hindsight unavailable to the early version of himself who lived them. Separated by time and depth of experience, the narrator can understand in ways that the character, immersed in the immediacy of events, cannot. This retrospective distance is evident in the introductory section when the narrator Sal's comments suggest a gap between his previous innocence and his current knowledge: "I could hear a new call and see a new horizon, and believe it at my young age" (10–11). And finally, there is the author, Jack Kerouac, whose relation to Sal Paradise appears at times purely transparent: Kerouac is Paradise, it sometimes seems, and *On the Road* is simply an autobiography with the names changed to avoid lawsuit. Yet for all its reliance on the facts of Kerouac's life and Kerouac's declaration "I hereby renounce all fiction" (*Letters,* 246), this remains a novel. The enormous overlap between author and narrator is evident, but Kerouac was free to alter the historical record whenever it suited his purpose, and it is not possible to collapse the distinction entirely.

On the Road opens on a note of despair: an unsuccessful marriage and a serious illness have left Sal "miserably weary," weighted down with a "feeling that everything was dead" (3). An earlier version included the death of his father as another sign of the dour condition, and all these details are autobiographical: Kerouac's brief marriage to Edie Parker had collapsed; not long after, his father Leo had died, and Jack himself had endured phlebitis. Despite the personal details, this dead-end feeling was not restricted to Sal (and Kerouac) at the time but reflected a somber and cautious mood in postwar America more generally. It was, as Kerouac put it elsewhere, a decade of "mediocrity and war" (*Letters,* 229). Yet a character named Sal Paradise—with its obvious echoes of salvation—must be destined to search for something beyond this cul-de-sac. Sal immediately announces his refusal to dwell on his unhappy circumstances, and the bleakness of these opening lines is quickly reversed. "With the coming of Dean Moriarty," he declares, shifting from a minor chord to a major, "began the part of my life you could call my life on the road" (3). This declaration stresses arrival rather than loss, beginning rather than ending, movement and energy rather than stagnation and death. Dean was born on the road, we are told, and it seems that Sal will be reborn there.

The road has been a central image in American culture and literature at least since Walt Whitman's celebration of it, and "going West to see the country" (3) has preoccupied Americans since the earliest European settlement of North America, driving the exploration and colonization of the continent. Sal's mood, then, speaks to a more general sense of immobility: in a recent study of Cold War culture, Alan Nadel writes that "the ubiquity of rule-governed society" fundamentally altered the American sense of possibility because it left "no river on which to flee, no western territory for which to light out."[3] While there were more cars and more drivers than ever, there was a corresponding decline in the possibility of escaping to any real frontier. Kerouac's friend Holmes noted a metaphoric connection between the Beat explorations and those of earlier, more literal, pioneers: "our immediate attraction to all those far-out experiences . . . [and] unexplored territories of consciousness," he writes, "exerted a pull on us fully as strong and as mysterious as the pull of the Far West a century earlier."[4] In anticipating Dean's arrival, Sal imagines a solution to the repressive condition of postwar American culture as well as to the stagnation of his own life.

When Dean arrives in New York, released from reform school and having worked for a time on a ranch in Colorado, Sal sees him in terms of this American frontier mythology: "My first impression of Dean," he states, "was of a young Gene Autry—trim, thin-hipped, blue-eyed, with a real Oklahoma accent—a sideburned hero of the snowy West" (5). Together, Sal and Dean seem to form a complementary unit: Sal, the cultured Easterner, appears to be a prisoner of his own thinking, physically free but tied in mental and emotional knots. Dean, on the other hand, the Western hero, is entrapped by reform school walls rather than by his own attitudes. His physical appetite is otherwise unconstrained, and his intellectual appetite—though unschooled—seems voracious. Sal can provide Dean with the literary, cultural, and intellectual direction he needs, and Dean can provide "something new" (10), the vitality and excitement, the spontaneity and impulsiveness that Sal lacks. When they meet, some explosive release of energy seems inevitable. The sense of containment reflects both a postwar mood and a longstanding American preoccupation. Dean's desire to live "without modified restraints" (7) is, in one way or another, as old as American literature and culture itself. Like his literary ancestor Huck Finn, another representative of natural freedom emerging from the lowest social classes, Dean is always in trouble; and like that 1950s icon of rebellious youth—the juvenile delinquent—he lives dangerously on the social edges, abjuring conventional and legal restraints.

Dean differs from many outsider figures, however, in combining lawlessness with a love of literature and philosophy as complementary aspects of a general project of personal liberation. Before coming to New York, "he'd spent a third of his time in the poolhall, a third in jail, and a third in the public library" (7). The poolhall/petty criminal lifestyle is not usually connected with frequent and excited visits to the library. More typically, the library is the site of an ascent to the middle class. Education is most often seen as the key to upward mobility, and following the war military service provided access for many young men to higher education and social advancement. But Dean seems to have no interest in upward mobility; instead he wants to bring knowledge down to where he is. Sal is fascinated by this odd combination, this inversion, and the sense of freedom that results. With the exception of the petty criminal hipsters he had come to know, "All my other current friends were 'intellectuals,' " Sal comments, putting the word in quotes to signal his mistrust of the concept. Dean is equally intelligent, but free of the "tedious intellectual-ness" of the others. The intellectuals in his circle of friends, like Sal himself with his bleak outlook at this point, "were in the negative, nightmare position of putting down society and giving their tired bookish or political or psychoanalytical reasons" for their alienation. Far from resonating with images of alienation or intellectual preten-sion and upward mobility, Dean reminds Sal of an idyllic American male youth "of old companions and brothers under the bridge, among the motorcycles, along the wash-lined neighborhood and drowsy doorsteps of afternoon where boys played guitars while their older brothers worked in the mills" (10).

Dean's criminal behavior is interpreted by Sal as a positive rather than a negative attitude. Sal has met and befriended a number of "slinking criminals" and hipsters who have taken to the life and morality of the streets and learned to survive with a "hip sneer." But here again, Dean is very different: "his 'criminality' was not some-thing that sulked and sneered; it was a wild yea-saying overburst of American joy" that cannot be stifled by legal convention. His criminal acts, then, are not comparable to those of the other hipsters Sal knows: while they might steal to support drug habits, for example, Dean "stole cars for joy rides" (10). The phrase "joy ride" must be understood quite literally as an experience of joy, and joy—sponta-neous and unmanageable—seemed to be in scarce supply in the sad world Sal describes. While victims of his crime might not be disposed to bother with such subtle distinctions, Sal insists that criminality resulting from an overflow of natural desire must be considered differ-ently—even as a kind of heroic act of resistance in a repressive world.

From this romantic perspective, the body's natural appetites can hardly be questioned, since "nature" is more fundamental than the intellectual apparatus from which any such questioning might pro-ceed. Dean thus appears as a "natural man," whose spontaneous energy and lust for life exist beyond need of justification, whose unaf-fected and unrepressed joyful hedonism provide an antidote to Sal's stagnation and intellectual preoccupation. This result of living in har-mony with natural rhythms is evident in Dean's appearance: "His dirty workclothes clung to him so gracefully, as though you couldn't buy a better fit from a custom tailor but only earn it from the Natural Tailor of Natural Joy" (10). This sentiment is hardly new in American literature of course: Henry David Thoreau, for example, early in *Walden,* warns his readers to "beware of all enterprises that require new clothes, and not rather a new wearer of clothes. If there is not a new man, how can new clothes be made to fit? If you have any enterprise before you, try it in your old clothes."[5] And Huck Finn, of course, like Dean, greatly prefers his comfortable old rags to the good clothes Aunt Sally provides.

Dean's transformative energy has the power to alter the mundane, make it extraordinary, invest it with an aura of excitement. As a parking lot attendant, Dean "worked like a dog" while dressed "in greasy wino pants with a frayed fur-lined jacket and beat shoes that flap." This situation is not an inspiring one, yet Sal's account elevates it to the heroic: "The most fantastic parking-lot attendant in the world," writes Kerouac, adding a breathless description of Dean's manic but expert pace:

> he can back a car forty miles an hour into a tight squeeze and stop at the wall, jump out, race among fenders, leap into another car, circle it fifty miles an hour in a narrow space, back swiftly into tight spot, *hump,* snap the car with the emergency so that you see it bounce as he flies out; then clear to the ticket shack, sprinting like a track star, hand a ticket, leap into a newly arrived car before the owner's half out, leap literally under him as he steps out, start the car with the door flapping, and roar off to the next available spot, arc, pop in, brake, out, run; working like that without pause eight hours a night. (9)

The glamour that envelops Dean is sufficient to negate the fact that he is in ragged clothes and doing menial labor. In fact, we begin here to see an inverted social hierarchy that elevates the antimaterialistic, down-and-out Beats above those who actually own the cars.

"He was," comments Sal, "simply a youth tremendously excited with life" (6), and this energy is manifested in all his activities. The gap between the visionary Dean and average Americans is suggested in the way they react to him in public places as an "overexcited nut." The category of the madman on the street, one of the extreme forms of marginalized eccentricity, is one that few aspire to or admire; in fact, it evokes in many a sense of mingled pity, disgust, and fear. From the other side, however, as Sal sees it, a sense of freedom results from the abandonment of the need to fit in. As he watches Sal write, Dean's response is impassioned; he yells "Yes! That's right! Wow! Man!" and mops his sweating face with a handkerchief as though writing were an exciting performance art. When Dean speaks of a new approach to writing, his prescription could apply to all areas of his life, including the religious, the domestic, and the sexual. "Man, wow, there's so many things to do, so many things to write! How to even *begin* to get it all down and without modified restraints and all hung-up on like literary inhibitions and grammatical fears." Released from these blockages even as he speaks of them, Dean projects a "holy lightning… flashing from his excitement and his visions" (7). In this cautious postwar period, treating the act of writing in such impassioned fashion was certainly innovative, and it was in fact Neal Cassady who inspired Kerouac's experiments with "spontaneous prose."

Dean's desire for intellectual stimulation—for "Nietzsche and all the wonderful intellectual things"—is combined with an unrepressed sexuality: "to him sex was the one and only holy and important thing"(4). Born on the road and raised on the edges of skid row by an alcoholic father, Dean has never been conditioned to accept the neurotic and repressive civility of middle America, the cultural pressures of propriety and guilt. His sexuality is represented as a spontaneous expression of physical pleasure, an appetite as natural as the desire for food: "so long's I can get that lil ole gal with that lil sumpin down there tween her legs, boy," he declares, and "so long's we can *eat,* son, y'ear me? I'm *hungry,* I'm *starving,* let's *eat right now!*" (10). The corollary, of course, is that he has learned to be neither responsible nor honest with his lovers. As the narrative progresses, however, the romantic impression of Dean as the possessor of a coherent identity based on natural and joyous desire is strained beyond the breaking point by the contradictions of his desires.

However misogynistic it may sometimes appear in *On the Road,* the notion of sexual potency as a sign of health—personal or cultural—is an old and well-used literary metaphor. In the area of psychoanalysis, the theories of Freud concerning sexual repression and of Wilhelm Reich—very influential among the early Beats—on the importance of orgasm were much discussed in postwar intellectual circles. While some of the attitudes toward gender and sexuality expressed in *On the Road* are difficult to defend, it is important to note the conditions that produced them. Dean's "natural" sexuality seemed a radical antidote to the repression, hypocrisy, and consumerist conditioning of postwar suburban conformism. This is the period in which the condemnation of pre- and extramarital sexuality coincided with the invention of the Playboy bunny, the proliferation of Hollywood starlets and sex queens such as Marilyn Monroe and Jayne Mansfield. No clearly articulated feminist critique was generally available, and the reduction of women to sexual objects was neither uncommon nor controversial as it is today. Dean Moriarty is one of the period's most influential examples of a widespread phenomenon that Barbara Ehrenreich has termed "the collapse of the breadwinner ethic," a repudiation of standard gender roles that "had begun well before the revival of feminism and stemmed from dissatisfactions every bit as deep, if not as idealistically expressed."[6]

Dean's relationship with "his beautiful little sharp chick Marylou" reflects both the spontaneity and passion that Sal finds so refreshing and the misogyny that many contemporary readers find so difficult to accept. With the word *chick,* Kerouac resorts to a hip language that—surprisingly—only occasionally surfaces in this classic Beat novel. A "chick" and a "wife" seem almost to be contradictory terms, and the details immediately suggest that this is no typical American marriage. Hungry after the long trip, they buy "beautiful big glazed cakes and creampuffs" despite their poverty. A taste for the impulsive and for the immediate gratification of desire is revealed here, for thrills without regard for the costs or the consequences, and this abandonment of Freud's reality principle in favor of the pleasure principle is soon confirmed as Sal enters the cold-water flat where Dean and Marylou are staying to find them making love on the couch while the apartment's real occupant is in the kitchen (4)—not the last time Sal would interrupt Dean this way.

Kerouac's narrative is very much focused on the situation of men, and women are not portrayed with much clarity or insight. As a result, it is difficult to gain a clear image of Marylou. Sal initially includes her in the same mythic frame that structures his image of Dean as a Western hero: "Marylou was a pretty blonde with immense ringlets of hair like a sea of golden tresses; she sat there on the edge of the couch with her hands hanging in her lap and her smoky blue country eyes fixed in a wide stare because she was in an evil gray New York pad that she'd heard about back West." But in the space of one paragraph, the image is altered until any coherent idea of Marylou evaporates. First her country innocence is transformed to the cosmopolitan and sensual ("a longbodied, emaciated Modigliani surrealist woman in a serious room"), and then this image dissolves into the demystified and dismissive: "outside of being a sweet little girl, she was awfully dumb and capable of doing horrible things." Dean and Marylou seem to live by a different set of rules than most normal couples, and yet postwar gender roles are maintained: at the end of an impromptu all-night party, for example, Dean "decided the thing to do was to have Marylou make breakfast and sweep the floor" (5). It is not easy to bring all these characteristics together into a unified image, and when—by the end of the page—Marylou is described as a whore, these apparently contradictory elements of the feminine mystique refuse coherence. Identity is often a difficult category in *On the Road,* but this example is an extreme case of the instability.

Marylou's willingness to break the gendered behavior codes constraining women at the time is not credited, and indeed she is dismissed as little more than a sexually attractive but occasionally dangerous nuisance. The pattern of unhappy heterosexual relationships contrasted with more satisfying male friendships is common in American literature, and in a matter of days, this volatile relationship blows apart when Dean flees their apartment after a fight. While Sal relegates Marylou's calling the police to vindictiveness and hysteria, reports of Dean's violence suggest that she may in fact have had good reason to complain. But after this split, Dean calls her a "whore" and begins a deepening relationship with Sal. When Sal, who is recovering from the breakup of his marriage, gets together with Dean, fresh from the breakup of his, a powerful form of male bonding occurs that is tested throughout the novel but never surpassed. Dean turns up at Sal's aunt's house to visit, and like Huck Finn, who has to get away from Aunt Sally, Sal and Dean go out to cement their relationship over "a few beers because we couldn't talk like we wanted to talk in front of my aunt" (6).

For Dean, this male "madness" (6) is incompatible with domesticity, and monogamy is not a workable arrangement, since the compromises and postponements it entails conflict with his need for spontaneous gratification and impulsive action. Tracing the male bonding pattern back to Cooper, Melville, Twain, and others, Fiedler analyzes a pattern "in which a white and a colored American male flee from civilization into each other's arms" (Fiedler, 12). Sal certainly feels that he must "light out for the territories" if he is to maintain his integrity, and Dean Moriarty, born and raised on the edges of the culture, performs a function similar to that of the "colored American." As Fiedler points out, "the figure of the natural man is ambiguous, a dream and a nightmare at once" (26), and while Sal usually sees Dean in the positive dream state, there is no doubt that the other side exists. Kerouac is typical of American writers in seeking "the last horizon of an endlessly retreating vision of innocence—on the 'frontier,' which is to say, the margin where the theory of original goodness and the fact of original sin come face to face" (27). These aspects come together but are not finally resolved in Dean, a man whose apparent lack of a sense of evil allows him to commit a variety of crimes, including violence and betrayal, on the frontier of culture.

The intensity of their relationship is displayed one evening as Sal works on his novel and Dean entices him out into the wilder world of New York nightlife: "Come on man," he urges, "those girls won't wait, make it fast" (*Road*, 6). Inspired at the thought of a night on the town with Dean, Sal races to finish, producing some of his best work. Leaving the pressures of work and the compromises of domesticity behind, they set out for the city "to meet some girls." But the real excitement seems less to involve "girls" than their own male relationship: "we leaned on each other with fingers waving and yelled and talked excitedly" (6). They understand each other well, and as a result, they "got along fine—no pestering, no catering" (7)—a tacit reference to the relationships with women they feel to be too fraught with constraints. The fact that when they arrive in New York, they find no "girls"—typical of the novel's false starts and wrong leads—is incidental, since the real excitement has been between the two of them anyway. The subsequent meeting with Carlo marks an even greater intensity, although Kerouac omits direct reference to the sexual aspect of the relationship that developed between Cassady and Ginsberg.

While Sal regrets not having Dean to himself, this episode begins an important process. "The whole mad swirl of everything that was to come began then," observes Sal, and "it would mix up all my friends and all I had left of my family in a big dust cloud over the American Night" (8). As they talk excitedly and exchange stories, they plant the seeds for an alternative subcultural community that would develop in years to come.

> Carlo told him of Old Bull Lee, Elmer Hassel, Jane: Lee in Texas growing weed, Hassel on Riker's Island, Jane wandering on Times Square in a benzedrine hallucination, with her baby girl in her arms and ending up in Bellevue. And Dean told Carlo of unknown people in the West like Tommy Snark, the clubfooted poolhall rotation shark and cardplayer and queer saint. He told him of Roy Johnson, Big Ed Dunkel, his boyhood buddies, his street buddies, his innumerable girls and sex parties and pornographic pictures, his heroes, heroines, adventures. (8)

In this exchange begins a mythology and a cast of characters that grew and evolved over the next 25 years as America learned to live with a major subculture that gradually transformed into a counterculture. And Sal—as much chronicler as participant—signals from the outset the eventual decline of this excitement: "They rushed down the street together, digging everything in the early way they had, which later became so much sadder and perceptive and blank. But then they danced down the street like dingledodies, and I shambled after as I've been doing all my life after people who interest me" (8). Against the backdrop of death, illness, and confinement that the opening pages invoke, Sal makes clear the focus of his interest:

the only people for me are the mad ones, the ones who are mad to live, mad to talk, mad to be saved, desirous of everything at the same time, the ones who never yawn or say a commonplace thing, but burn, burn, burn like fabulous yellow roman candles exploding like spiders across the stars and in the middle you see the blue centerlight pop and everybody goes "Awww!" (8)

The passage is perhaps the most frequently quoted of all of Kerouac's writing, no doubt because it articulates the ecstatic sense of intensity that ignited this group and fascinated the whole country. Yet it is rarely recalled that this is tightly linked to a much bleaker feeling that, according to Sal, inevitably follows—"sadder and perceptive and blank" (8). Two sides of the coin of psychological intensity, these states define the emotional spectrum for Sal, and those more mundane moments in between are not worth investigation.

While specific to this moment in American history, a postwar moment of surface conformity and underlying anxiety, this feeling is not historically unique but is common to many generations coming of age and wishing to throw off the weight of tradition. "What did they call such young people in Goethe's Germany?" (8) Sal wonders as he marvels at the intensity of the need to talk, to write, to experience, and to learn. As the reference to Goethe demonstrates, every generation is alike in that it must, to some degree, interpret its own coming-of-age and try to project the mythology it will live by. Like Goethe, whose early novel *The Sorrows of Young Werther* set the style for a generation of young people, Kerouac played an important part in the developing identity of postwar American youth confronting an unprecedented set of historical circumstances that strained continuity, a strain that became known as "the generation gap." In the 1990s, it is difficult to imagine a single novel having the impact of *Werther* or *On the Road,* but this dynamic of identity formation is still played out in literature, music, and film.

Sal does not attempt to emulate Dean—something he could never accomplish in any case. Instead, Dean's adventurous energy and openness to chance sets a precedent that opens the door for Sal to begin his own exploration of America and of himself. When Dean heads west, Sal vows to follow: "I promised myself to go the same way when spring really bloomed and opened up the land" (9). More urgent than any self-doubts or warnings from his aunt is the sense of quest, ill-defined though it be: "Somewhere along the line I knew there'd be girls, visions, everything; somewhere along the line the pearl would be handed to me" (11). The image of the pearl is an ancient one, a symbol without precise reference but implying wisdom, purity, and beauty; and it is an appropriate object of Sal's quest once he heeds Whitman's advice (at the end of "Song of the Open Road") to "Let the paper remain on the desk unwritten" and take to the open road. "So, leaving my big half-manuscript sitting on top of my desk . . . I left with my canvas bag in which a few fundamental things were packed and took off for the Pacific Ocean" (11–12).

The narrative that follows—in keeping with the spirit of the road itself—is episodic, picaresque rather than densely structured or deeply plotted, replete with wrong turns, unexpected adventures, and roads that lead nowhere. And while there are "girls" and "visions," there is no clear moment when the pearl is handed to him. Joyce Johnson has argued that Kerouac's real concern was with voice, and as a result "his 'true life' novels often seem defiantly plotless."[7] While there is no question that Sal learns a great deal in his time on the road, it would be difficult to construct this novel as a traditional narrative of continuous growth toward some definitive knowledge or epiphany in the way that the pearl image suggests. While there are many moments when some ultimate insight is announced or some final identity proclaimed, none lasts, and the novel ends less on a note of achieved wisdom than with an admission of the vanity of such ambitions.

Typically, the eventual catalyst for his departure is a promise that remains unfulfilled: a letter from his friend Remi Boncoeur (Henri Cru), who holds out the Melvillean lure of a job on a ship and a voyage around the world. The job never materializes—only one of Sal's expectations that remain unrealized. Whatever his original reasons for venturing out, whatever his maps and plans assert, the road does not always lead where Sal thinks. Whitman would, of course, be quick to distinguish the road itself from maps of the road and plans for travel—and this is Sal's first mistake. "I'd been poring over maps of the United States in Paterson for months, even reading books about the pioneers" he reports (12). As is the case with so much of the detail in the novel, it is quite autobiographical. While living with his mother in Ozone Park, New York, Kerouac studied American history as well as collecting and studying maps before setting out on the first of the journeys that make up this narrative. In a 1947 letter, Kerouac wrote: "I have begun a huge study of the face of America itself, acquiring maps (roadmaps) of every state in the USA, and before long not a river or mountain peak or bay or town or city will escape my attention. . . . My subject as a writer is of course America, and simply, I must know everything about it" (*Letters*, 107). If his project is, at least in part, a reclamation or reinvention of the "wild selfbelieving America" he believed to have existed in his grandfather's time and before, a spirit that seemed to have disappeared in recent years, then American history is a valuable resource ("Origins," 59). But the best-laid plans of armchair travelers, pioneers of the imagination, often go astray, and for all his fine planning, Sal ends up lost and isolated on his first day out.

Echoing *Walden,* Thoreau's classic of American nonconformism, Kerouac begins his main narrative. "In the month of July 1947, having saved about fifty dollars from old veteran benefits, I was ready to go to the West Coast" (11). Thoreau, describing the beginning of his experiment writes, "Near the end of March 1845, I borrowed an axe and went down to the woods by Walden Pond"(Thoreau, 27). But Sal's new start seems already compromised by its commencement date. Having promised to set out "when spring really bloomed" (9), his departure—unlike Thoreau's—is delayed until July, midsummer. Contrasting further with Thoreau's air of confidence and control is Sal's account of the difficulties he runs into almost immediately, difficulties that result from his inexperience and suggest that the pearl ought not be taken for granted.

Still, it is a beginning. Sal chooses Route Six, which, "on the roadmap was one long red line . . . that led from the tip of Cape Cod clear to Ely, Nevada, and there dipped down to Los Angeles" (12). Dreaming of the adventures to come, he sets out across an America that maps and books could never prepare him for. The purity of his dream and plan is challenged as his ideals are tested and transformed by the world's tendency to puncture idealism, to confound plans with complex actuality. "If you drop a rose in the Hudson River at its mysterious source in the Adirondacks," Sal considers as he sets out by the Hudson River himself to begin his hitchhiking, "think of all the places it journeys by as it goes out to sea forever" (12). While he appears willing to submit to the flow of the river here, his understanding of what this might mean will change as the novel charts his course. This sense of abandonment to the flow of experience is soon tempered: a thunderstorm, pouring rain, Sal in sandals, and little traffic on this remote stretch of road force him to begin rethinking his imaginary America. "High up over my head the great hairy Bear Mountain sent down thunderclaps that put the fear of God in me. All I could see were smoky trees and dismal wilderness rising to the skies. 'What the hell am I doing up here?' " he asks himself (12). His shoes—"huaraches, plantlike sieves not fit for the rainy night of America and the raw road night" (13)—betray the fact that his studies and his bohemian city life have not prepared him well for this.

One detail here that deserves close attention is the reference to "the rainy night of America." This phrase recurs later, most often with reference to the Mississippi River rather than the Hudson, but the image of the rain and the river flowing to the sea constitutes one of the most significant in the novel. When the novel ends, Sal is beside another river on another night, thinking about some of the same problems, but with a great deal more resignation in his voice. "It was my dream that screwed up," he decides, summing up this false start in retrospect, "the stupid hearthside idea that it would be wonderful to follow one great red line across America instead of trying various roads and routes" (13). Abstract knowledge gleaned from history books and maps allows the imagination to reduce complex reality to straight lines and clear directions that experience will inevitably confound, rendering his sense of the poetry of travel, his song of the open road, somewhat less rhapsodic: "I swore I'd be in Chicago tomorrow, and made sure of that, taking a bus to Chicago, spending most of my money, and didn't give a damn, just as long as I'd be in Chicago tomorrow" (13). The irony of Sal's inauspicious beginning is heightened by contrast with the nineteenth century writers who seem not to have confronted such blockages. Heading back to New York to catch a Chicago bus, he travels with a group of schoolteachers whose conversation he finds uninspiring—"chatter-chatter blah-blah" (13). It is difficult to imagine Whitman's mythic traveler in such banal straits, Thoreau taking a crowded bus to Walden Pond, or Melville's Ishmael distressed by being caught in the rain on his way to board the Pequod. Nevertheless, the following day finds Sal on the road at last, but with less sense of romance: "It was an ordinary bus trip," he writes, "with crying babies and hot sun, and countryfolk getting on at one Penn town after another" (14).

This deflationary episode is one of the first to contribute to Sal's education. There is a naïveté in his sense of quest ("girls, visions, everything") appropriate perhaps to the sensibilities of a young man setting out at that time to explore himself and the world, and Kerouac has been criticized for the tone of lines such as this. Fiedler, for example, writes of the novel's "bohemian-kitsch" tone, and asserts that "The fact that one is tempted, even impelled to speak of such a writer as Kerouac at thirty-five as a 'boy' " indicates an immaturity of tone and content (Fiedler, 289–90). This sort of criticism is often made of *On the Road*, suggesting that the line between Sal as character (naive) and Sal as narrator (experienced) is not always clear. Tim Hunt makes the case that "the tension between the competing claims" of the two Sals, one embodying "hindsight" and the other "exuberance" (7), is the central dynamic of the novel (Hunt 1996, 7). If he was naive in dreaming of "pearls" and "girls" at the outset, and if his shifting and deepening awareness is central to the novel, then some clearer indication of his revised attitude might be expected. There is no question that a gap exists between the two Sals, but it is easy to make too much of this point in an effort to attribute to the novel a traditional linear coherence that it may not in fact possess or even aspire to.

In recounting Sal's brief stay in Chicago, Kerouac touches on a crucial aspect of Beat culture: community. Alone in this large city, staying at the YMCA, Sal ventures for "one long walk after midnight into the jungles" (14), an urban frontier zone beyond the safety and conventionality of the white mainstream. In his solitude, he is even followed by police, a detail confirming his socially marginal status. Yet his mood is far from alienation: "And as I sat there listening to that sound of the night which bop has come to represent for all of us, I thought of all my friends from one end of the country to the other and how they were really all in the same vast backyard doing something so frantic and rushing about" (14). This episode occurs not long after Richard Wright's *Native Son,* set in Chicago, electrified the reading public with a narrative of racial oppression and violence—yet for Sal the threat seems to emanate more from the police than from the residents. This somewhat menacing police presence recurs throughout and is related to the notion of repression, one of the novel's dominant themes.

Norman Mailer, in his influential and controversial essay "The White Negro," published around the same time as *On the Road,* argued that for those who could not or would not fit in, the obvious recourse was to precisely such frontier zones in large cities where safe predictability had not yet penetrated and polite respectability had not yet triumphed. For Mailer, the choice was clear: "One is Hip or one is Square," he asserts, "one is a rebel or one conforms, one is a frontiersman in the Wild West of the American night life, or else a Square cell, trapped in the totalitarian tissues of American society."[8] Mailer's essay alludes directly to Thoreau's sense of "quiet desperation," placing it in the context of existentialism and postwar angst, and suggesting that in the shadow of Hiroshima and Auschwitz a solution lies not in a Thoreauvian retreat to rural isolation but in adopting the new and radically oppositional stance of the urban "hipster."

The music of this frontier zone was bebop: "At this time, 1947, bop was going like mad all over America" (14). Musicians such as Charlie Parker, Dizzy Gillespie, and Thelonious Monk had taken jazz in new directions, and Kerouac was an early enthusiast. Among whites particularly, the number of bebop fans was not great at this point, and those who did appreciate its daring innovations and dazzling flights of individual virtuosity often had, not surprisingly, much else in common as well. For this group, bop had come to represent the freedom, excitement, and danger of the urban night in which it appeared. With African American sources, bop crystallized a sense of alienation from the middle-class values and lifestyle of postwar America; and in its astonishing solos, it provided a powerful image of restless individual creativity, endless resourcefulness and control out on the edge. In foregrounding the solo and encouraging the soloist to push the limits of the form, it seemed to provide an antidote to what Kerouac regarded as the decline of "wild selfbelieving individuality" in postwar America. Prior to this time, jazz had been shifting to the safe commercial forms of big-band swing and, LeRoi Jones argues, bebop was a deliberate attempt "to restore jazz ... to its original separateness, to drag it outside the mainstream." In mainstream America, "bebop fell on deaf or horrified ears," but there was a group of alienated white Americans who recognized this "willfully harsh, anti-assimilationist sound" as their own.[9]

In the first Beat novel, *Go* (1952), Kerouac's friend John Clellon Holmes, an acute observer of the Beat scene, describes this subculture, its perils, and preoccupations: it was a world

> of dingy backstairs "pads," Times Square cafeterias, be-bop joints, night-long wanderings, meetings on street corners, hitchhiking, a myriad of "hip" bars all over the city, and the streets themselves. It was inhabited by people "hungup" with drugs or other habits, searching out a new degree of craziness; and connected by the invisible threads of need, petty crimes of long ago, or a strange recognition of affinity. They kept going all the time, living by night, rushing around to "make contact," suddenly disappearing into jail or on the road only to turn up again and search one another out. They had a view of life that was underground, mysterious, and they seemed unaware of anything outside the realities of deals, a pad to stay in, "digging the frantic jazz," and keeping everything going.[10]

This New York scene was not unique. There were, of course, other bohemian groups scattered across America, but no sense of a national cultural pattern emerged until such works as Ginsberg's "Howl" and Kerouac's *On the Road*—as bebop itself had done—provided symbolic rallying points. *On the Road,* whatever its status in relation to traditional canons and literary genres, was enormously important in the formulation of a more cohesive subcultural identity whose ramifications could not have been predicted. This sense of new possibilities on the horizon, of the collapse of old taboos and an emerging potential for new cultural forms that might refute America's exclusionary racial logic, redefined high and low culture, sacred and profane experience, provided an excitement in this postwar subcultural group that harked back to the ferment of the 1920s. With this reflection, Sal truly begins his journey: "for the first time in my life, the following afternoon, I went into the West. It was a warm and beautiful day for hitchhiking" (14). Ironically, this voyage, which came to represent the idea of freedom for so many, begins in the shadow of a prison. Followed by a police cruiser the previous night, Sal passes Joliet penitentiary on his way "out of the impossible complexities of Chicago traffic" to the open highway.

5

The First Journey

Following Sal's frustration in New York and his difficulties getting out on the road itself, this section expresses a joyful—and more success-ful—abandon to the risk and chance of the hitchhiker's road. His first ride takes him into "great green Illinois" (14) on roads that "shoot west for incredible distances" (15). The next goes much farther: "I was all for it. Iowa!" he declares. The simple thought of Iowa is not often sufficient to arouse in travelers an exclamation mark, but for Sal, student of maps, it is a situation of great pleasure to say the word, to possess the image, and then to arrive at the reality. *On the Road* dis-plays a frequent tension between representation and reality, and often Sal experiences satisfaction, even joy, to find the two harmoniously resolved. The same occurs as he arrives at the banks of the Mississippi, the road of Sal's literary ancestor Huck Finn, the preeminent water-way of American mythology: "And here for the first time in my life I saw my beloved Mississippi River, dry in the summer haze, low water, with its big rank smell that smells like the raw body of America itself because it washes it up" (15). The river, here described as a cleansing agent, will be the subject of extended meditation later in the novel when it comes to figure importantly in Sal's "myth of the rainy night."

As he moves across the Midwest, his fascination with scenes of ordinary American life becomes clear. "All the men were driving home from work, wearing railroad hats, baseball hats, all kinds of hats, just like after work in any town anywhere" (15). This blue-collar working world was one Kerouac knew well, having grown up in that atmosphere himself. After his time at Horace Mann Prep School and Columbia University, his experience with the bohemians and intellectuals of New York, he returns to the subject of working-class America with a nostalgia tinged sometimes with joy, sometimes with sadness. The truck drivers demonstrate this: as one "balled that thing clear to Iowa City" and another "balled the jack and told stories for a couple of hours," Sal joins in "with [his] soul whoopeeing," exclaiming "was I happy!" (16). As the miles roll past, one driver tells of how he eludes the law, "Them goddam cops can't put no flies on *my* ass," he declares (16), providing a glimpse of the freedom from constraint and surveillance that Sal has been seeking. In contrast, Sal's ride into Des Moines seems flat. It is "a ride with two boys from the University of Iowa; and it was strange sitting in their brand-new comfortable car and hearing them talk of exams as we zoomed smoothly into town" (17). These middle-class students are categorized as "boys," and neither their car nor their conversation evokes Sal's interest: clearly Sal's search for "the mad ones" need not linger in such zones of comfort, security, and respect for authority.

As he travels, the transitory nature of experience becomes increasingly evident. Rather than trying to make his life follow a well-planned course, Sal lets events occur—as any hitchhiker must. Rides may come quickly and easily or take many hours; a ride may go one mile or a thousand. When a car pulls over for a pick-up, neither driver nor rider can predict the chemistry of their relationship. An attractive offer—a ride going all the way to Los Angeles—may tempt him from his Denver destination, or it may not. At one point, a carnival owner stops and offers him work—an opportunity that could take his life in a sudden new direction, but he declines the offer. Life on the road is a life of hazard, chance, and being on the road entails a willingness to accept whatever arbitrary circumstances turn up. The road experience forces a continual disruption, a juxtaposition of contrasting perspectives, and stemming in part from this, in Des Moines, Sal experiences an identity crisis.

This crisis is foreshadowed when, during a rest stop, Sal goes for a "walk along the lonely brick walls illuminated by one lamp, with the prairie brooding at the end of each little street" (16–17). The sense of a vast darkness outside the perimeter of the human settlement provides an image of the limits of safety and knowledge. His desire for a new life transgressing those limits leads to the radical disorientation that overcomes him. Having gone to sleep in the daytime, he wakes at sunset and finds himself in a brooding prairie darkness of his own:

> that was the one distinct time in my life, the strangest moment of all, when I didn't know who I was—I was far away from home, haunted and tired with travel, in a cheap hotel room I'd never seen ... [I] really didn't know who I was for about fifteen strange seconds. I wasn't scared; I was just somebody else, some stranger. (17)

This deconstructive moment occurs, as Sal notes, "halfway across America, at the dividing line between the East of my youth and the West of my future." And while it seems to represent a profound turning point, it is not entirely clear whether the result is the founding of a new identity for the West and the future, or whether Sal has embarked on a course that leads to the erosion of identity. As the journeys continue, Sal adopts many roles and identities, but none ever really seems to hold, to provide the solidity it initially appears to promise. This is the first of several moments of identity crisis, part of what Jonathan Paul Eburne sees as an "attempt to drain identity of its fixity," an ultimately subversive strategy to destabilize the "coercive standards" of Cold War America.[1]

This condition is suggested again in Shelton, Nebraska, where Sal and his current hitchhiking companion Eddie are delivered by "an old man who said nothing" (21). The tone is set by Eddie, standing "forlornly in the road in front of a staring bunch of short, squat Omaha Indians who had nowhere to go and nothing to do" (21). The exclusion and alienation of Native Americans forms part of the novel's larger image of the situation of all those on the margins of America's postwar dream of upward mobility. Suddenly Eddie remembers being in Shelton before, on a train heading west in wartime. The train stopped "late at night when everybody was sleeping. I went out on the platform to smoke, and there we was in the middle of nowhere and black as hell, and I look up and see that name Shelton written on the water tank. Bound for the Pacific, everybody snoring, every damn dumb sucker. . . . Damn me, this Shelton! I hated this place ever since" (21–22). This wartime experience seems linked, coincidentally perhaps but nonetheless forcefully, to the aimless lives of the Indians, to the silent old man who brought Sal and Eddie there, and to the fact that their motion is impeded here as they are unable to get another ride. Eddie's Shelton posits an image of modern American life as a nocturnal prairie train ride through nowhere, taking conscripted passengers to some oblivion.

Just as Sal's personal identity is dissolving, his sense of public America is challenged by new realities. At Council Bluffs, he recalls, "All winter I'd been reading of the great wagon parties that held council there before hitting the Oregon and Santa Fe trails; and of course now it was only cute suburban cottages of one damn kind and another, all laid out in the dismal gray dawn" (19). The old America is disappearing, and the "wild selfbelieving" American spirit that Kerouac valued so highly has been eroded between the era of the frontier and the era of the suburb, between the wagon train and the tourist sedan. The worst cars to hitchhike, he observes, are the tourist cars "with old men driving and their wives pointing out the sights or poring over maps, and sitting back looking at everything with suspicious faces" (22). Sal himself has pored over maps and risked letting the map obscure reality, but now he is focused on the world around him rather than representations of it. Still, in spite of his enthusiasm for the West, it seems that the spirit he is searching for is no more prevalent here than in the East: "Tall, sullen men watched us go by from false-front buildings; the main street was lined with square boxhouses. There were immense vistas of the plains beyond every sad street" (27).

One possibility is available in the cowboy, a figure still suggesting an ideal of American manhood on the margins of mainstream middle-class culture. Dean Moriarty is described as a cowboy when he arrives in New York, for example, and Sal's first sighting of a contemporary cowboy elicits recognition: "walking along the bleak walls of the wholesale meat warehouses in a ten-gallon hat and Texas boots, [he] looked like any beat character of the brickwall dawns of the East except for the getup" (19). Both cowboy and Beat maintain a distance from suburban existence and the "cute" comforts of modernity in an attempt to preserve some older individual integrity; here though, in the modern suburban frontier, the cowboys too find themselves surrounded by brick walls. The image of cowboys—America's heroes—adrift in a modern world that has no place for them recurs in many forms as Cold War culture evolved: in Hollywood movies such as *The Misfits* and *Midnight Cowboy*, or such Paul Newman movies as *Hud* and *Hombre*, for example, the image of the anachronistic or anti-heroic cowboy is used to speak to a more general sense of alienation, enervation, and enclosure in the modern world. Kerouac here anticipates the way that the Beat and the cowboy would serve as related figures of modern alienation in the popular imagination. Chad King's father provides Sal with an exemplary case of this decline. As a boy "on the North Dakota plains in the eighties...he rode ponies bareback and chased after coyotes"; now he pursues litigation over royalties on a cleaning product he once developed (39–40).

The experience is not all negative though, and traces of the "wild selfbelieving" spirit can still be found. At a roadside diner, Sal encounters a man with "the greatest laugh in the world," a man who might have emerged from an earlier, freer, and healthier America: "here came this rawhide oldtimer Nebraska farmer with a bunch of other boys into the diner; you could hear his raspy cries clear across the plains, across the whole gray world.... He didn't have a care in the world and had the hugest regard for everybody" (21). The man impresses Sal simply with his presence, his vitality, not his intellect or sophistication. His laughter and banter bring out the best in everyone present, penetrating even the gray world of the new suburban West. Kerouac renders his accent faithfully in order to note its eccentricity, its divergence from standard English.

"Maw, rustle me up some grub afore I have to start eatin myself raw or some damn silly idee like that." And threw himself on a stool and went hyaw hyaw hyaw hyaw. "And thow some beans in it." It was the spirit of the West sitting right next to me. I wished I knew his whole raw life and what the hell he'd been doing all these years besides laughing and yelling like that. Whooee, I told my soul. (21)

This eccentricity is highly prized; it is not the self-conscious nonconformism that later became the "beatnik" trademark but the genuine and unaffected difference that could flourish far from urban centers.

It is no tourist car that takes Sal to Cheyenne, but the "greatest ride in my life," a ride on a flatbed truck without safety rails with "the most smiling, cheerful couple of handsome bumpkins you could ever wish to see, both wearing cotton shirts and overalls, nothing else; both thick-wristed and earnest, with broad howareyou smiles for anybody and anything that came across their path." Their policy of picking up every hitchhiker they pass ensures the eclectic nature of the crowd in the back of this truck. Once on board, Sal swigs "rotgut . . . in the wild, lyrical, drizzling air of Nebraska," as someone else yells, "Whooee, here we go!" (24). Just as he became excited at the mere thought of Iowa, here the atmosphere of Nebraska, through the transformative power of Sal's vivid imagination, becomes "wild, lyrical." While he finds something of interest in all the riders, the most notable is Mississippi Gene, "a dark little guy who rode freight trains around the country, a thirty-year old hobo but with a youthful look so you couldn't tell exactly what age he was." When he speaks, the words are "melodious and slow," and he and his traveling companion wear "hobo rags . . . old clothes that had been turned black by the soot of railroads and the dirt of boxcars and sleeping on the ground" (25).

His bearing suggests a quiet wisdom borne of marginal experience that is as important to Sal in its way as the frenetic energy of Dean: "he sat on the boards crosslegged, looking out over the fields without saying anything for hundreds of miles" (25). Here, as in Shelton, the prairie fields exude a sense of nothingness, of the sublime, and Gene is perhaps a counterpart of Conrad's Marlowe in *Heart of Darkness,* who also sits cross-legged and looks out. But while Marlowe sees into a space of horror, Gene gazes out in this emptiness with equanimity. Gene's wisdom is the wisdom of the "wise and tired old Negro" (28), making him—to borrow Mailer's phrase—one of Kerouac's "white negroes," a voluntary exile from what Sal sees as the deceptions and delusions of white culture. Like Melville's Bulkington in *Moby Dick*, the man who eschews the comfort and security of home, his life is a constant journey: "crossing and recrossing the country every year, south in the winter and north in the summer, and only because he had no place he could stay in without getting tired of it and because there was nowhere to go but everywhere, keep rolling under the stars" (28). The meditative, even mystical, suggestions raised by his cross-legged posture are confirmed in the way he looks out in a "Buddhistic trance over the rushing dark plains" (30) and asks questions ("Where *you* headed?" [25]) that intimate deeper levels of significance. Part Buddha, part "wise old Negro," part hipster (28), Gene proves that other ways of life do continue outside the increasing uniformity of the American mainstream. "I was astounded," Sal exults as darkness falls, "I yelled for joy. We passed the bottle. The great blazing stars came out, the far receding sand hills got dim. I felt like an arrow that could shoot out all the way" (27).

This emerging set of oppositions between straight America and another spirit found on its fringes is further clarified in Cheyenne—a town whose name is taken from Native culture. They arrive during Wild West Week, a modern festival trading on the legendary history of the West. It is clear that the passengers on that truck, not the Wild West Week party-goers, are the legitimate descendants of the Old West, transients in their own version of a covered wagon. "And the truck left, threading its way through the crowds, and nobody paying attention to the strangeness of the kids inside the tarpaulin, staring at the town like babes from a coverlet. I watched it disappear into the night" (33). With this watchfulness, Sal establishes himself again—as his comments on Council Bluffs suggested—as a guardian of some more authentic American spirit that, banished from the suburbs, belongs now out in the space beyond. There is certainly no place for it in the Wild West Week revelry, an event more parodic than celebratory. "Big crowds of businessmen, fat businessmen in boots and ten-gallon hats, with their hefty wives in cowgirl attire, bustled and whooped on the wooden sidewalks of old Cheyenne." Among the crowded saloons and the sound of blanks being fired off, Sal considers the situation: "I felt it was ridiculous: in my first shot at the West I was seeing to what absurd devices it had fallen to keep its proud tradition" (33).

Sal's first dramatic misreading of America occurred when his map-study led him to Bear Mountain and a highway leading nowhere. At that point, he confronts a geography his reading did nothing to prepare him for, a primal nature whose landscape and weather overwhelm his knowledge. In Cheyenne, the opposite takes place. He is prepared for an elemental America, the America of the pioneers and the frontier spirit, but encounters instead its replacement by shallow copies of the original as "the fat burpers were getting drunker and whooping up louder" (34). The only witnesses to another reality, besides the riders who stared from the truck as they disappeared into the night, are the alienated Native Americans, "really solemn among the flushed drunken faces...Indians, who watched everything with their stony eyes" (34–35). For Sal, the most incisive critical gaze on modernity's reductive and dehumanizing power is located among the hoboes and the transients, lumpenproletariat and racial outcasts.

Sal has been a witness too, and looking forward to his arrival in Denver ("Wow! What'll *Denver* be like!" [37]), he imagines the impression he will make on his friends as he arrives with the experience of the road behind him: "in their eyes I would be strange and ragged and like the Prophet who has walked across the land to bring the dark Word, and the only Word I had was 'Wow!' " (37). According to Nicosia, Kerouac's (or Sal's) "Wows" constitute "one of the book's mantras," but phrases such as this one contribute to the impression of immaturity that many readers have noted (Nicosia, 328). Hunt argues that at this point, Sal is "a college boy on a lark" and that his attitudes are "naive and open to ridicule" (Hunt 1996, 11). The self-conscious projection of prophetic identity seems little more than idle daydreaming; there has been nothing about this trip sufficient to qualify him to speak as "the Prophet" who brings the "dark Word." If there is a subsequent voice of experience to lend another perspective to this naïveté, it is not immediately evident.

This moment is one of many heavy with the promise of a significance that is never really made manifest, a hint of finality that is never borne out. Considering his actual arrival in Denver, where no further mention is made of his prophetic calling, this fantasy establishes Sal's desire for coherent identity and transcendent vision much more than it provides a sense that he possesses either. Part of this elevated language is no doubt connected to Kerouac's belief that the "naturalistic" language predominant in this century—by this he seems to mean the reductive language of rationality—"is the cause of all the trouble" (*Letters*, 176). In this 1948 letter to Ginsberg, he states his opinion that people are "godlike" and in the narrative he often emphasizes the mythic dimensions of the characters, deliberately choosing an excessive and naive language in order to reintroduce myth and wonder in an age of disenchantment.

Sal's first image of Denver replaces the artificiality of Cheyenne's Wild West Week with the seedy reality of Denver's skid row, another kind of wild west. "I stumbled along with the most wicked grin of joy in the world, among the old bums and beat cowboys of Larimer Street" (37), the setting for Dean's early life when, as son of "one of the most tottering bums," he would "beg in front of Larimer alleys and sneak the money back to his father, who waited among the broken bottles" (38–39). Given Dean's subsequent development, this environment exists as a privileged site for the Beat mythology of the margins Sal is engaged in creating. But his first social contacts in Denver are with another, more "normal" group he meets through Chad, the person who originally introduced Sal and Dean in New York. Chad has since developed new interests and friends, however, becoming interested in anthropology, particularly involving precolonial Native America. Chad, in his excitement, seems uninterested in the present, while Sal, as his encounter in Cheyenne indicates, is more interested in identifying with alienated Indians than in studying them.

Chad's friends include Roland Major, with whom Sal stays for the next few days in a "really swank apartment" (40), a strong contrast to the poverty of Larimer Street. Major, wearing a silk dressing gown, writes "Hemingwayan" stories about people saddened that "arty types were all over America, sucking up its blood" (41). Major, an "arty type" himself, is likeable enough, but the contradiction of his position seems clear: there is no solution here to the disease that seems to be afflicting America. Major's incantatory proper nouns are European and imply a class-specific connoisseurship: "Ah, Sal, if you could sit with me high in the Basque country with a cool bottle of Poignon Dix-neuf." But Sal's nouns are American, and identify a very different class imagination: "I love boxcars and I love to read the names on them like Missouri Pacific, Great Northern, Rock Island Line. By Gad, Major, if I could tell you everything that happened to me hitching here" (41). Both of these characters establish positions outside bourgeois America, but Major's seems to lead to the dead end signified in his stories, while Sal's offers more space to explore, more raw energy to tap. As Kerouac explained to Holmes, he was having to choose between "the drawing rooms full of Noel Cowards and the rattling trucks on the American highways"(McNally, 126).

When they travel to Central City, this contradiction becomes even clearer. Like so much of Sal's American West, it is a monument to past glory rather than a site of contemporary possibility. Once the site of a rich silver find, this boomtown even boasted an opera house attracting international stars before becoming a ghost town and later, a tourist attraction. Like Cheyenne, it has become little more than an imitation of reality: "It was a big vacation for everybody. Tourists came from everywhere, even Hollywood stars. We drove up the mountains and found the narrow streets chock full of chichi tourists" (51). As he attends a performance of the opera in a borrowed suit, now turned into a tourist himself, Sal considers the startling shifts of his fortunes: on skid row a few days ago, "now I was all racked up sharp in a suit, with a beautiful well-dressed blonde on my arm, bowing to dignitaries and chatting in the lobby under chandeliers. I wondered what Mississippi Gene would say if he could see me" (52). In spite of Sal's exhilaration, Gene represents a kind of uncompromising integrity that betrays the artificiality of all this, undercutting Major's affectation with a dose of unaffected integrity. Sal's strongest sympathies are with this side of the social world, the Beat spaces of Dean and Gene and others like them, and he feels himself having to make a choice: "I wished Dean and Carlo were there—then I realized they'd be out of place and unhappy" (54). His developing sense of Beat identity becomes clear as he thinks of them "rising from the underground, the sordid hipsters of America, a new beat generation that I was slowly joining" (54). This understanding of a Beat underground derives from many sources, ranging from the New York hipsters to French bohemians to Dostoyevsky's Underground Man, a major literary influence at the time.

While this group identity was enormously important, both for Kerouac and for the emergence of sub- and countercultural identities in ensuing decades, there is another important point raised here that the novel continues to explore: the instability and impermanence of identity. In the space of a few days Sal moves from skid row to "swanky apartment," from hitching rides with down-and-out transients to a chandeliered opera theater. The remarkable fluidity of these shifts, determined more by chance than by deliberation, suggests the radical instability of identity that Kerouac foregrounds. In a letter to Cassady, Kerouac writes of the social pressure to "look right"—that is, to fit in. Those who fit in are safe: "no cop, no prick dares question their freedom. It's all an evil game. I change faces a hundred times a day in knowledge and aversion of this" (*Letters*, 213). While it had its practical benefits, Kerouac's ability to "change faces" and assume a variety of identities also seems to be related to his lack of a stable and secure identity underlying these social camouflage roles. "Kerouac," Ginsberg once noted, "was not heavily entangled in such fixed identities" and could imaginatively take on successive personae—one of many characteristics he shares with Sal.[2] In his letters, Kerouac repeatedly announces decisive actions and choices that have little or no impact: new career moves, love interests, writing projects all announced with ringing finality then promptly forgotten. This very movement—the continual reinvention of the self juxtaposed with a deep and apparently contradictory desire for stability—is itself a crucial theme of the novel.

With Dean and Carlo, his "sordid hipster" friends, Sal seems more connected. Dean and Carlo are the "underground monsters of that season in Denver" (39), a fact symbolized, as Sal points out, by the basement apartment that served as a meeting place. Sal's first Denver meeting with Dean, "a new kind of American saint," rehearses the first New York meeting when Sal disturbed Dean and Marylou (4): this time, Dean opens the door "stark naked. I saw a brunette on the bed, one creamy thigh covered with black lace, look up with mild wonder" (43). Inspired partly by Dean, a frantic round of partying begins, lasting several days and culminating in Sal's symbolic inversion: "I jumped out [of the car] and stood on my head in the grass. All my keys fell out; I never found them" (45). This carnivalesque image conveys a sense of the world upside down, normal values and responsibilities overturned, the abandonment of old spaces and the acceptance of new. One Beat literary ancestor, poet Arthur Rimbaud, wrote of the systematic disordering of the senses as a path to understanding, and—as Kerouac acknowledges—this path was explored extensively by the Beats.[3] The relative normality of Major's "swanky" apartment stands in contrast to the intensity and abnormality of Carlo's "underground" room where the "whole universe was crazy and cockeyed and extremely strange" (47).

Visiting this room is an almost allegorical voyage into premodernity, with echoes of the Dostoyevsky novels Kerouac and the others were reading: "You went down an alley, down some stone steps, opened an old raw door, and went through a kind of cellar till you came to his board door. It was like the room of a Russian saint: one bed, a candle burning, stone walls that oozed moisture, and a crazy makeshift ikon" (47). The peculiarity of the place is accentuated by the conversation taking place between Carlo and Dean, their attempt to establish a total and absolute honesty. When Carlo says, "There's one last thing I want to know—" Sal counters, "That last thing is what you can't get, Carlo. Nobody can get to that last thing. We keep on living in hopes of catching it once and for all" (48). This is perhaps the closest Sal comes to the prophet position he had foreseen, but instead of bringing "the dark Word" (37), he argues now that the Word cannot be spoken, that finality is not a possibility.

Carlo refers in his poetry to the Rocky Mountains as papier-mâché, but as Sal leaves at dawn, the Colorado landscape brings a larger perspective to bear on these facile words: "I walked out and took a trolley to my apartment, and Carlo Marx's papier-mâché mountains grew red as the great sun rose from the eastward plains"

(50). This is not so much the utterance of the Word or the consolidation of a myth as an acknowledgment of the sublimity of nature in relation to the language of humans. A few pages later, when Sal goes up into those mountains, he considers again the relationship of human discourse to nature: "I wondered what the Spirit of the Mountain was thinking" of all this craziness "as we fumed and screamed in our mountain nook, mad drunken Americans in the mighty land. We were on the roof of America and all we could do was yell" (55). At this moment, in Sal's imagination a prophetic figure is approaching to fulfill the same function he once thought he could fulfill: "an old man with white hair was probably walking toward us with the Word, and would arrive any minute and make us silent" (55). These two images, the first denying the possibility of final meaning and the second fantasizing its delivery, demonstrate Sal's conflicted quest. There are many moments when this quest seems on the brink of fulfillment, when the "pearl" seems within his grasp, yet before long he is lost as ever. Awakening the next morning in a dirty room, Sal finds the window nailed shut and vision impeded. "We coughed and sneezed. Our breakfast consisted of stale beer.... Everything seemed to be collapsing" (56), and as the frenzied activity subsides, Sal is struck with the sadness that follows him in all his travels.

As Kerouac's comments about the ill-effects of "naturalistic" language suggest, some language ought to be available for the discussion of these large questions, even if the Word remains out of reach. Before departing for San Francisco, Sal spends a night with Rita Bettencourt, and while their sexual encounter seems a disappointment, it is their unsatisfying discussion that seems to preoccupy Sal more. Rita appears to be the antithesis of the exciting people ("desirous of everything at the same time, the ones who never yawn or say a commonplace thing") who, Sal has said, attract him. When he asks her what she wants from life, she yawns. "I put my hand over her mouth and told her not to yawn" (57). Later, Sal lies down with the hoboes on the lawn of a church and considers the sadness of modern romance and its lack of an adequate language. "Boys and girls in America have such a sad time together; sophistication demands that they submit to sex immediately without proper preliminary talk. Not courting talk—real straight talk about souls, for life is holy and every moment is precious" (57). While traditional courtship rituals hold no appeal, Sal regrets that modern sexuality lacks a vocabulary equal to its significance and so results in a sense of sadness and loss.

An odd juxtaposition of circumstances here is related to Kerouac's desire to reinvest modern life and sexuality with a sense of the holy: these ideas neither occur to him inside the church nor impel him to enter. Instead, considerations of holiness are located in the churchyard among hoboes who periodically panhandle change from passersby, suggesting the startling degree of Sal's alienation from the mainstream of American culture and that culture's distance from any sense of holiness. This lack of an adequate religious framework was, for Kerouac, an important problem not only in sexuality, but in all areas of life. In a letter to Ginsberg at this time, Kerouac discusses some lines from a poem Ginsberg had sent him: "Sad paradise it is I imitate, / and fallen angels whose lost wings are sighs." The first words may have inspired Sal Paradise's name, according to Ann Charters, and the sadness itself, Kerouac argues, is directly related to the loss of the holy and of a sense of sacrament, the condition of "fallen angels" (*Letters*, 120–21). Preparing to leave Denver, Sal wanders around Denver's seedy side just as he had on arrival, and the image portrays humanity—fallen angels all—clustered around "sad honkytonks... movie marquees, shooting parlors" while "[b]eyond the glittering street was darkness, and beyond the darkness the West" (58).

Sal's next stop places the West quite literally beyond the darkness as he arrives in San Francisco around dawn. In Mill City, he stays with Remi Boncoeur, whose surname *Boncoeur* means "good heart," and Sal remarks that Remi "had a heart of gold" (63). The stay in Mill City, according to Sal "the only community in America where whites and Negroes lived together voluntarily" starts out with great promise: "so wild and joyous a place I've never seen since" (60). The joy is apparent, for instance, in Remi's laugh. Like the laugh of the "Spirit of the West" (21), it is "one of the greatest laughs in the world," a laugh of Rabelaisian proportions: "he leaned on the wall and laughed and cried, he pounded on the table so you could hear it everywhere in Mill City, and that great long 'Aaaaah' resounded around the canyon" (61).

51

Later, he unleashes a laugh that "roared over the California woods and over America" (71–72). Remi's laugh rivals that of his next-door neighbor, "a Negro called Mr. Snow whose laugh, I swear on the Bible, was positively and finally the one greatest laugh in all the world" (62). Mr. Snow's laugh is theological in scope: "he got up, apparently choking, leaned on the wall, looked up to heaven, and started; he staggered through the door, leaning on neighbors' walls; he was drunk with it, he reeled throughout Mill City in the shadows, raising his whooping triumphant call to the demon god that must have prodded him to do it" (62). Kerouac refers to Rabelais in his letters at this time, and his use of hyperbole throughout *On the Road* owes something to "the divine tricks" he learned there (*Letters,* 205).

In spite of all this, Remi is in some difficulty with Lee Ann, his attractive but "sharp-tongued" lover who alternates between hating Remi and Sal and being bored by them (62–63). Her only interest in Remi is based on her erroneous belief that he will inherit a great deal of money. When Remi and Sal lose their money at the racetrack, the division between men and women that emerged clearly with Sal and Dean in New York is reasserted: the men are willing to laugh at the whole misadventure, but Lee Ann, apparently vindictive like Marylou, is unwilling to forgive or forget. Sal dislikes Lee Ann and her mercenary and bitter attitudes—she even hates Mr. Snow and his laugh: "I get so sick and tired of that sonofabitch" (74). Yet—typical of Kerouac's conflicted attitudes toward women—he is also attracted to this "fetching hunk" (62), even fantasizing about running off with her (73). This pattern of attraction to the lovers of his male friends was recurrent in Kerouac's own life. In fact, his first wife, Edie Parker, had been the fiancée of Henri Cru, Kerouac's friend since prep school and the man on whom the character of Remi is modeled. Lee Ann is even less likeable than Marylou and, like her, never takes on the qualities of a rounded character whose point of view can be grasped. Once again, in Kerouac's work women tend to obstruct male friendships and freedom.

If heterosexual relationships constitute one aspect of conventional living that Sal cannot deal with easily, another is work. It is not easy to imagine a job for which Sal is less suited, but he soon takes on police work, and this draws out one of the novel's central themes: the conflict between desire and repression. This is a clear step away from the direction he had been taking, toward joining "the sordid hipsters of America" and he wonders how his Beat friends will react (63). The men he has to guard, captives of an exploitative system, are being sent to Okinawa to work for a year—in much the same situation as Eddie, who had his moment of dark epiphany in Shelton, Nebraska (21–22). They are "tough" and "shifty" men, many "running away from something—usually the law," and "knowing full well how horrible it would be . . . they drank" (64). Sal's job is to contain this resistance, to ensure "that they didn't tear the barracks down." Throughout the novel, Sal is himself seeking a way to escape the social constraints that limit individual creativity and freedom. But now, he becomes an agent of the very forces of repression he has tried to elude. The conflict represented here is essentially the same one Kerouac referred to in a 1949 letter to Cassady in which he discusses the fear caused by "the American Gestapo that hounds the American Dispossessed . . . the poor, the beat, the 'characters' " (*Letters*, 213).

The guards were "a horrible crew of men, men with cop-souls" (64) who actually look forward to making arrests. One looks back fondly on the time he spent as a guard at Alcatraz: "We used to march 'em like an Army platoon to breakfast. Wasn't one man out of step. Everything went like clockwork" (66). Another, festooned with weapons, ammunition, and leather, looked "like a walking torture chamber" (67). This vision of order does not sit well with Sal, who identifies more with those being guarded than with the guards. Indeed Sal and Remi themselves resort to theft in order to supplement their incomes, and Remi in particular becomes adept at stealing groceries from the very company that employs them to guard against such violations. One night, Sal, an ineffective guard at best, fails to control the men, gets drunk with them instead, and in the morning raises the American flag upside down—a blatant sign of disorder. "You can't compromise with things like this," warns one guard, "Law and order's got to be kept" (67). The best moments on the job for Sal, however, are connected to drinking with those he is supposed to be guarding or else carrying on with Remi. In a letter at the time, Kerouac wrote that, responding to a call, "Henri Cru and I rushed out with our clubs, guns and flashlights, laughing like hell and goosing each other on the way" (*Letters,* 114).

"This is the story of America," Sal observes, generalizing from this situation to the postwar condition. "Everybody's doing what they think they're supposed to do. So what if a bunch of men talk in loud voices and drink the night?" (68). Sal's anarchic desires take him far from this regimentation of the human spirit. What he really wants to do is get away from this stifling paramilitary atmosphere, to "sneak out into the night and disappear somewhere, and go and find out what everybody was doing all over the country" (67). In a letter to Cassady, written while on duty, Kerouac admits the absurdity of his situation, and makes a plea: he asks that his friend not "think ill of me for being a cop": "I do *not* do my duty.... I stare at the women on the grounds, fingering my genitalia, and move on shuffling my feet" (*Letters,* 113). This persona made Kerouac more uncomfortable than most, it seems, yet he manages to continue to subvert authority even while wearing its uniform.

In another letter, written to Ginsberg the same night, Kerouac discusses wearing another kind of costume, displaying another manifestation of his tendency to identify with the guarded rather than the guards. He and Henri look for clothes, abandoned by workers who have left for Okinawa, that they can keep. Along with stealing food, this is a way of supplementing their wages. "Thus the parade of suits, smelling of stale sad whiskey and the ends of night, Skid Row, puke, sperm, and sadness" (*Letters,* 121). In these filthy clothes, Kerouac maintains a connection to the Beat spirit of dispossession even while acting as the agent of its repression, an extremely conflicted form of identity. This "dressing up" suggests the trying on of such abject identities—returned to later in the novel in a Detroit skid-row movie theater—as Kerouac and the Beats discovered an America that could not easily be assimilated by the new social order. This America was filled with "demographic 'others,' " observes Eburne, "down-and-outs, drug addicts, homosexuals, criminals, political subversives, and other such undesirables against whom the National Security State was protecting itself, as well as the jazz legends, hipsters, and African Americans whom the U.S. refused to recognize" (Eburne, 68–69). It is here, on the frontier of an unrecognized America, that Sal's identity crisis and search for possibility take place.

As a guard, Sal's repression of desire has unexpected consequences as well. One such incident, involving his police gun, occurs as Sal's erotic frustrations with women ("I tried everything in the books to make a girl") turns his attention to the sexual availability of gay men:

> There were plenty of queers. Several times I went to San Fran with my gun and when a queer approached me in a bar john I took out the gun and said, "Eh? Eh? What's that you say?" ... I've never understood why I did that; I knew queers all over the country. It was just the loneliness ... and the fact that I had a gun. I had to show it to someone. (73)

If the description of Sal's time with the police is taken as an extended comment on the nature of repression, then this incident demonstrates the fact that desire and repression are not simple categories. The mixture of an explicit threat of antigay violence with barely concealed desire, of the evident phallic imagery of the gun with a denial of understanding, suggests the existence of a complex pattern of attraction and repulsion that Kerouac apparently preferred not to investigate further. Despite the very autobiographical—almost confessional—content of *On the Road,* and despite the importance of gay sexuality to Kerouac and to a number of his male friends, this whole area remains more or less repressed.

While Kerouac himself had numerous homosexual experiences throughout his life, he was never able to resolve this aspect of his sexuality. In a 1945 letter to Ginsberg, he refers to the "remorse and disgust" he felt after such encounters, relating it to his repressive upbringing. He complains about the gay lifestyle, but seems ambivalent, even confused, about his own desires. The "physical aspects," he states, "disgust me consciously." Beyond that, "I cannot be too sure ... whatever's in my subconscious is there. I am not going to play the fool about that. My whole waking nature tells me that this sort of thing is not in my line. It keeps on telling me. It drums in my nature, telling me, until I begin to suspect its motive" (*Letters,* 97). In a 1948 letter to Cassady he returned to this subject, and it remained a complicated issue. "I consider queerness a hostility, not a love," he writes, connecting homosexual desire to "envy, hostility, aggression, and inverted desire." Yet even in expressing these attitudes in a private letter, he is already conscious of protecting his reputation in a homophobic society. These remarks are directed to " 'posterity' which might someday read this letter.... Posterity will laugh at me if it *thinks* I was queer ... little students will be disillusioned" (*Letters*, 167). This difficulty continued to plague him for years. Later in his life, as his alcoholism progressed, he developed a tendency to rage against homosexuality even while continuing to have male sexual partners.

The episode in Mill City highlights the dissident mentality developing in postwar America in the midst of its militarization and increasing repression of difference. Kerouac highlights his own irresponsible behavior because it is one of the few available forms of resistance, a refusal to fall into line, much less force others into line. As Gifford and Lee maintain, Kerouac's position "was subversive without being political."[4] His attempt was not to change the system, a hopeless prospect at that time, but to escape from it, and Kerouac looked both to the historical past and to the contemporary social margins for images of freedom from modern conformism and the pressure of orderly obedience. His alternatives often seem less than politically progressive, but to him progress signified modernity's continuing move toward the further alienation of the human spirit. This position has echoes of Mailer's assumption in "The White Negro" that no political recourse was available at a time when both left (Stalinism) and right (fascism or McCarthyism) appeared to lead to totalitarianism. Kerouac's interest in skid row, then, was predicated not on a belief that a social solution might lie in this hopeless direction but on a refusal of the bright and shallow comforts of his culture—a refusal that would in a few years become known as "dropping out." One of Sal's first actions upon leaving Mill City and its constellation of confusing and unpleasant circumstances is to have "a beer among the bums of a saloon" (79). With this symbolic gesture, he is "on the road again."

On a bus to Los Angeles Sal meets Terry, a Chicana migrant worker who clearly is an outsider, a representative of that cultural community Kerouac often referred to as the "fellahin": she has a young son, is married to an abusive man, and lives with her family "in a shack in the vineyards" (82). Their relationship, Sal's happiest with a woman, is one of the defining moments in the novel, and Gerald Nicosia argues that Kerouac's relationship with Bea Franco (the model for Terry) was a crucial one for Kerouac as well. "He had crossed a great divide in his own life. Until that point all his crazy deeds, even taking drugs, were things a Lowell boy might do—however much he'd be censured for them. But a white boy from Lowell didn't live with a brown-skinned Mexican.... [She] introduced him to a beater world than he had known"(Nicosia, 200). The term *fellahin* was derived from Oswald Spengler's monumental work *The Decline of the West*, and Spengler's view of history was much discussed among Kerouac and his friends. An early friend and intellectual influence, Sebastian Sampas, first recommended it to him (*Letters*, 65), and Burroughs subsequently encouraged the early Beat group to study it as well (Gifford and Lee, 38). Later in his life, according to Tom Clarke, as Kerouac tried to understand the furor his novel had unleashed, he turned back to this vast study of the patterns of world history.[5]

Originally signifying Arab peasantry, the term is extended by Spengler to include one of the three groups in his historical "morphology of peoples."[6] The first stage, the primitive, refers to the early stages of culture; the second category includes those imperial cultures that arise to dominate the historical stage. The *fellahin* is the third term and refers to those largely "primitive" groups who are marginalized by "civilization" during its ascendancy and who remain little changed when the empire ends its historical trajectory in collapse. In the aftermath of civilization, "The residue is the *fellah* type" who occupy its ruins (Spengler, 105). Spengler thus sets up an opposition between the "historical peoples, the peoples whose existence *is world history*" on one hand and on the other the fellahin, those whose lives are postcivilization, posthistorical. Whereas the lives of the former are imbued with meaning and depth, legitimated and guaranteed by the imperial culture, "Life as experienced by . . . fellaheen peoples is just . . . a planless happening without goal . . . wherein occurrences are many, but, in the last analysis, devoid of signification"(Spengler, 170–71).

A curious thing begins to happen when an imperial culture goes into decline, according to Spengler: the intelligentsia, once leading the historic climb from the local and primitive to world significance and imperial dominance, gradually become *"spiritual leaders of the fellaheen."* In their rejection of the official narrative of national destiny, these "cosmopolitan" literary intellectuals begin to identify with those living on the margins of the imperial culture. As the numbers of such intellectuals—"world-improvers" Spengler calls them dismissively, historical "wasteproducts"—increase, so is the ultimate demise of the culture assured (Spengler, 185). Spengler's conservative and pessimistic vision was enormously influential and can be found echoed in many cultural documents of the first half of this century. Kerouac recognized himself in this description, but with a major difference. The image of the postimperial, postcivilization, postcolonial—indeed postmodern—life of planless happening shared by fellahin and intellectuals that Spengler disparages as insignificant, Kerouac, inversely, admired and desired to emulate—at least at the outset of his career. The Beat Generation's philosophy and style, he argued, was really a recuperation of the premodern culture of

> Western mankind before it went on its "Civilization" Rationale and developed relativity, jets and superbombs had supercollassal [*sic*], bureaucratic, totalitarian, benevolent, Big Brother structures. So, as Spengler says, when the sunset of our culture (due now, according to his morphological graphs) and the dust of civilized striving settles, lo, the clear, late-day glow reveals the original concerns again. ("Aftermath," 49)

It seems to Sal at this point that these original concerns could be better addressed in the company of a woman who has not herself become accustomed to the comforts and compromises of middle-class modernity. "You could have all your Peaches and Bettys and Marylous and Ritas and Camilles and Inezes in this world," says Sal (82), dismissing the women he has met in favor of this woman from a far more marginalized culture. Nicosia argues that Kerouac's relationship with Bea Franco was quite opportunistic: "in a ruthless way he was just having an experience." While Terry was a migrant Chicana worker in a racist nation, "his own salvation was only as far away as the nearest Western Union office, from which he could wire his mother for money to get home"(Nicosia, 200–201). It is important to remember too, as Nicosia indicates, that such a relationship was far more unlikely then, when the boundaries segregating the "fellahin" were far more rigidly enforced. And while Kerouac may have seen this idyllic tryst more as a literary subject than as a real relationship with a real woman, it certainly appears to have been as satisfactory—albeit brief—as any of his relationships with women.

Their initial attraction is immediately challenged as they emerge in the city, "the ragged promised land, the fantastic end of America" (82). Suddenly they begin to revert to cultural stereotypes: Sal thinks Terry is a prostitute setting him up to get mugged and Terry suspects Sal of being a pimp luring her into prostitution. These "foolish paranoiac visions" were "all a fit of sickness" (83) comments Sal in retrospect, but at the time (as now) these images all too often had the power to affect recognition across such starkly drawn racial lines as existed between white America and its racial others—and indeed, Kerouac himself succumbed to this racial hysteria in his later years. But finally these "two tired angels ... hung-up forlornly in an L.A. shelf" resolve their apprehensions and make love "in the sweetness of the weary morning" (84). This relationship has ramifications for Sal's continuing quest for self, allowing him to absorb, almost osmotically, elements of the forlorn "fellahin" identity he craves.

Later, as they explore "the loneliest and most brutal of American cities," Sal notes the "cop-soul" in operation again as "Booted cops frisked people on practically every corner" (85). Yet here, even more than in Mill City, the forces of order are unable to contain the anarchic vitality. The neighborhood "was a fantastic carnival of lights and wildness" peopled with the "beatest characters in the country" (85), and Sal's rhapsodic description of the passing scene captures its energy, the eclectic mixture of marginal people who animate it. The air is filled with the pleasurable smells of marijuana, chili, and beer, and the grand wild sound of bop floated from beer parlors; it mixed medleys with every kind of cowboy and boogie-woogie in the American night.... Wild Negroes with bop caps and goatees came laughing by; then long-haired brokendown hipsters straight off Route 66 from New York; then old desert rats, carrying packs and heading for a park bench at the Plaza; then Methodist ministers with raveled sleeves, and an occasional Nature Boy saint in beard and sandals. I wanted to meet them all, talk to everybody. (86)

The period that follows is one of the most intense and idyllic intervals in the novel, as Terry introduces Sal to a world off-limits to most whites. "I was ready for anything," declares Sal (87), and hungry for life outside the white mainstream, he soaks in the atmosphere of the "dark alley behind Mexican kitchens," the "chickenshacks barely big enough to house a jukebox"—but the jukeboxes are filled with Sal's favorite music: blues, bop, and jump. He visits Terry's friends, who live "up dirty tenement stairs"—Margarina, "a lovely mulatto," and her husband, "black as spades and kindly." Sal enjoys their gracious hospitality, their playful and affectionate children, and the atmosphere wafting up from Central Avenue, "the wild humming night ...[that] howled and boomed along outside. They were singing in the halls, singing from their windows, just hell be damned and look out" (87–88). Unlike many before and since, this account of the inner city represents it as a site of freedom rather than of violence, of humanity and excitement rather than ignorance and misery.

Sal's tendency to identify more and more with Terry's culture is clear as they attempt to hitch a ride one night only to be passed by cars full of jeering and cheering young people returning from a sports event and amusing themselves by taunting what they take to be a Chicano couple. "I hated every one of them," Sal declares, "little high-school punks ... [whose] parents carved the roast beef on Sunday afternoons" (88). The situation is worsened when Sal and Terry encounter them later: "they saw that Terry was Mexican, a Pachuco wildcat; and that her boy was worse than that" (89)—a white who has, in their eyes, sunk below his racial place. But this moment of identity confusion—the first of several—points toward precisely the transformation Sal seeks, one that takes him into a "fellahin" space offering the closest thing to hope that the novel can project. This downward social mobility is illustrated when Sal and Terry drink wine in the railroad yards with the hoboes: "Ah it was a fine night," Sal lyrically recalls, "a warm night, a wine-drinking night, a moony night, and a night to hug your girl and talk and spit and be heavengoing" (90). Terry offers love, but does not constitute an obstacle to the Beat/hobo lifestyle he is exploring: "Anything I did was alright with her. . . . she wouldn't care" (90–91). In Denver, Sal left Rita to join the hoboes in the churchyard, but now he has found a woman who will accompany him. Sal is excited by the freedom of lowered expectations supposedly enjoyed by the "fellahin," but the hints are there from the beginning that this is merely a temporary arrangement: even as they sit drinking in the hobo space of the railroad yard, one of their happiest moments, Sal is already thinking of the moment he will say good-bye.

Their next move takes them to the cotton fields as pickers, familiar terrain for Terry but a novelty for Sal. The fact that Sal's description of this experience relies so heavily on clichés and stereotypes suggests the limited degree to which Kerouac was able, as a relatively privileged white man of his time, to understand the position of the "fellahin," and points to the fact that this interval is essentially the acting out of a fantasy. The pastoral scene is set as carefully as a landscape painting or a panoramic scene from one of the many Hollywood films the novel refers to. "It was beautiful. Across the field were the tents, and beyond them the sere brown cottonfields that stretched out of sight to the brown arroyo foothills and then the snow-capped Sierras in the blue morning air." Despite discomfort, Sal revels in his humble situation: "My back began to ache. But it was beautiful kneeling and hiding in that earth. If I felt like resting I did, with my face on the pillow of brown moist earth. Birds sang an accompaniment. I thought I had found my life's work." If this rhapsodic passage arouses doubts about the clarity of Sal's vision—there is little possibility even at this point that his "life's work" is that of a migrant field worker—it is nonetheless consistent with Kerouac's attempt to escape from American modernity. This escape to a timeless pastoral space leads, quite logically, to a piece of American racial mythology that could have come from *Gone with the Wind*: "There was an old Negro couple in the field with us. They picked cotton with the same God-blessed patience their grandfathers had practiced in ante-bellum Alabama; they moved right along their rows, bent and blue, and their bags increased" (96).

Coming when the Civil Rights movement was gathering force and about to emerge as the most effective social movement in American history, this image of ahistorical African American willingness to endure oppression is difficult to accept. Intellectuals and literary people such as Sal and his creator Kerouac would have been aware by 1957 when *On the Road* was published—if not when the experiences it chronicles actually occurred—of contemporary debates on the issues surrounding racial exploitation exposing the vicissitudes of racism sufficiently to disabuse anyone of such beatific imagery. But Sal, needing a space not integrated into middle class modernity, remains locked into his romantic pastoralism, and later, after a long hard day resulting in very little pay, he moves further into his role. "I looked up at the dark sky and prayed to God for a better break in life and a better chance to do something for the little people I loved" (96), he declares with a touch of unconscious condescension, momentarily forgetting that he has indeed had a much better break in life and that if he really wanted to do something for Terry and her son he could. This would, however, take him out of his "fellahin" role, and that is not the direction that interests him.

Instead, his imaginary identification is extended: "Sighing like an old Negro cotton-picker, I reclined on the bed and smoked a cigarette." At the moment when white America's racist exclusion of these groups from the benefits of modernity was about to face its most radical challenge, Kerouac seems to see this apartheid almost as a blessing in disguise since it protected these segregated groups from a modernity that he considered not only fundamentally alienating, but also on the brink of self-destruction. Whatever the merits of such an argument against modernity, it is clear that Sal's metamorphic identity posits a curious space of radical freedom precisely among those who, by any conventional reckoning, would be counted among the least free. For a while though, his immersion in the role appears absolute. He claims to have forgotten his previous life, his attraction to the road and his "hip" friends, and asserts the reality of his new identity: "I was a man of the earth, precisely as I had dreamed I would be." The fantasy culminates in another moment of identity confusion, albeit a positive instance rather than a moment of collapse. Other whites in the area "thought I was a Mexican, of course," Sal observes, "and in a way I am" (97). Earlier, it was only hostile strangers who misrecognized him, but now he too—briefly and mysteriously—adopts this mistaken identity as his own.

This idyll comes to an end when autumn chill arrives and Sal decides it is time to return to "real" life and for Terry to return to her place among "the great fellahin peoples of the world" (98). When money arrives from his aunt, his concern with the fate of the "little people I loved" quickly evaporates. He has had his adventure, is ready to move on, and has the means to do so: "The money was in; my aunt had saved my lazy butt again" (101). To be a man of the earth is not after all his "life's work" it seems, nor is Terry his "girlsoul" for more than a few weeks. From the beginning, Sal has been casting himself in various roles and constructing various scenarios, all of a temporary nature despite occasional claims to permanence. A property common to writers perhaps, but one which Kerouac possessed to an unusual degree, this mobile identity—with the road as a metaphor for this mobility—allowed him to explore a wide range of subcultural positions in search of an expanded space of white male possibility. While one may react to this chameleon quality with suspicion—Norman Podhoretz reacted by dismissing Kerouac's work as "know-nothing populist sentiment" (307) and more recently Simon Frith refers to his identification of and with African Americans as "weirdly racist" (180)—many readers responded to Kerouac's suggestion that there were many more ways to live than the white middle-class roles they were finding unsatisfying. In retrospect, as Ginsberg later commented, "we were in the middle of an identity crisis prefiguring nervous breakdown for the whole United States".[7] This somewhat schizoid sociality is reflected in Sal's uncertain grasp of his own identity, and if his attempts to reinvent himself at times seem clumsy and ill-considered—particularly with the benefit of several decades of hindsight—this ought not be too surprising.

One important factor in the succession of imaginary identities is the storehouse of imagery provided by the literature and movies frequently referred to in *On the Road*. Dean enters as Gene Autry with Marylou at his side as the country girl of innumerable movies (5). These images are not always useful though; as the fake cowboys in Cheyenne demonstrate, such representations can be false and demeaning. Alternatively, they can be so derivative as to drain reality away, as is the case with Roland Major's Hemingway persona and stories about artists "sucking up [America's] blood" (41). When Sal arrives in California, closer to Hollywood, the references to movies and books increase substantially: in Mill City he waves his gun around "like Charlie Chaplin" (63) and walks down "a road like in *The Mark of Zorro* and a road like all the roads you see in Western B movies" (64). At one point Sal sees "the ghost of the San Francisco of Jack London" (72), and Fresno appears as "Saroyan's town" (80). He and Terry arrive in Hollywood, according to Sal, at dawn, "like the dawn when Joel McCrea met Veronica Lake in a diner, in the picture *Sullivan's Travels*" (82). "Everybody had come to make the movies," Sal admits, "even me" (87).

Sal's attempt to find a place in the movie industry as a screenwriter may have failed, but his role-playing continues unabated as he drunkenly performs lines from "*Of Mice and Men* with Burgess Meredith" (90). Hollywood had become—and still remains—the central identity-bank of American culture. As he prepares to leave for the East, Sal sits on a wall in a Hollywood parking lot making sandwiches for his trip home and reflecting on his experiences in California: "As I labored at this absurd task, great Kleig lights of a Hollywood première stabbed in the sky, that humming West coast sky. All around me were the noises of the crazy gold-coast city. And this was my Hollywood career—this was my last night in Hollywood" (102). Sal's career in Hollywood may be over, but his tendency to slip into the various roles supplied by literature and popular culture is by no means over. This tendency is an indication of the attempt—sometimes selfish and desperate, sometimes creative and insightful—to invent new ways of being a white male in a culture whose list of available roles had become remarkably narrow and regulated.

Ironically, the search for finality, for points of origin, reality, and true identity frequently leads to more mirages—such as Sal's dream that he has finally become a man of the earth and that his problems are solved with this role. Just as Sal becomes confused by geographic images of the real America when planning his trip and becomes confused by historical images and myths of America as he travels, he has difficulty separating a real self from his images of selfhood. At times, it seems that he is struggling to get beyond this to a final self-knowledge; but his struggles often lead him further into a hall of mirrors and the very images he hopes will lead him out into reality only take him further in. One example of a man lost inside is the Ghost of the Susquehanna: an utterly confused old man, hopelessly astray, yet convinced he knows the way, "the little hobo stand[s] under a streetlamp with his thumb stuck out—poor forlorn man, poor lost sometimeboy, now broken ghost of the penniless wilds" (104). The word *forlorn*, literally meaning lost, appeared earlier, in Sal's description of his first night with Terry, and it occurs as well in the novel's final paragraph.

Sal has a glimpse of this lost condition himself—neither his first nor last crisis of identity—the next day when he is thrown out of the railroad station where he has been sleeping.

> Isn't it true that you start your life a sweet child believing in everything under your father's roof. Then comes the day of the Laodiceans, when you know that you are wretched and miserable and poor and blind and naked, and with the visage of a gruesome grieving ghost you go shuddering through nightmare life. I stumbled haggardly out of the station; I had no more control. All I could see of morning was a whiteness like the whiteness of the tomb. (105)

Kerouac alludes to a series of visionary or prophetic moments in part 1, beginning with Sal's image of himself as a prophet and continuing with the moment in Central City when Sal imagines an old man arriving with the Word (55). The ghostly vision here—particularly in juxtaposition with the lost and confused Ghost of the Susquehanna—echoes an apocalyptic tone that recurs in the novel suggesting that the revelation may not be a positive one. Knowledge may remain impossible, and the whiteness of the pearl, the original goal of his quest, may be exchanged for the whiteness of the tomb.

Sal arrives back in New York "sick and tired of life" (106) and surrounded suddenly with all the energy and activity of Times Square at rush hour. Ever mindful that the ultimate result of all this swirl is mortality, he surveys "the absolute madness and fantastic hoorair of New York with its millions and millions hustling forever for a buck among themselves, the mad dream—grabbing, taking, giving, sighing, dying, just so they could be buried in those awful cemetery cities beyond Long Island City." The birth of "Paper America" is thus juxtaposed with the death of human America, and Sal's Beat alienation is emphasized; as he wanders among the "high towers of the land . . . the place where Paper America is born," he is far below the high towers of commerce and bureaucracy, looking for cigarette butts on the sidewalk by a subway door (106). In a 1948 journal entry, Kerouac's distance from all this is clear: "In Russia they slave for the State, here they slave for Expenses. People rush off to meaningless jobs day after day, you see them coughing in the subways at dawn. They squander their souls on things like 'rent,' 'decent clothes,' 'gas and electricity,' 'insurance.' "[8]

Albeit with some difficulty, Sal returns home to his aunt and to his writing as the cold fall winds arrive. All his images of prophetic vision, the anxieties, nightmares, and experiments in identity and role-playing that propelled him while traveling are swept away as he eats and plans the purchase of a new refrigerator. In the flux of comings and goings, of "girls, visions, everything," he has missed Dean—the main inspiration for the journey—and forgotten to call Camille. There has been no identifiable moment when "the pearl" was handed to him, but his description of his aunt's rug-making suggests some new insight: it is "a great rag rug woven of all the clothes in my family for years, which was now finished and spread on my bedroom floor, as complex and as rich as the passage of time itself" (107). *Ragged* is one of the most-repeated, emphasized words in *On the Road's* description of the Beat condition, and in the rug we see that the rags of time, of experience and identity, can be woven together in complex but complete patterns. Whether Sal will achieve this unifying vision or be left with rags will be addressed in the novel's final paragraph, but for now it remains to be seen as his return to the safety of home brings to an end part 1 and Sal's first journey.

6

The Second Journey

Part 2 begins just after Christmas, more than a year since Sal's brief encounter with Dean in Denver. Sal's family Christmas contains little intimation of festivity: "gaunt men and women...talking in low, whining voices," exchanging "the general weary recapitulation" (109) of events that hold little interest for Sal. Dean's sudden arrival once again signals a kind of rebirth, however, as "utter confusion" (110) envelops the group. Having lived quietly for some months with Camille, as husband and father with a responsible railroad job, Dean "blew his top." He has withdrawn all his money from the bank, bought an expensive new car, abandoned Camille and their child, and headed east with Marylou and Ed Dunkel. Ed's wife Galatea began the trip but was left behind. In this section, a frantic male search for some ideal of ecstatic freedom is played out against the stabilizing forces of modernity.

Driving madly across the wintery continent, Dean resembled "a monk peering into the manuscripts of the snow" (112), an image imputing to Dean's manic behavior a higher quality. No longer simply a young man eager for kicks, in Sal's eyes Dean has embarked on a vast hermeneutical project and his "madness ... had bloomed into a weird flower" (113). By any normal standards, he is unacceptably irresponsible and self-absorbed, but from Sal's perspective he is on a quest too important "for scruples" (112), a notion Kerouac perhaps derived from Dostoyevsky, a major influence during this period. When Galatea (Ed's wife) ran out of money on the journey east, for example, "Dean and Ed gave her the slip in a hotel lobby and resumed the voyage alone ... and without a qualm" (111–12). Later, Dean concludes that God too "exists without qualms" (120). The suggestion is that Dean has, in a godlike fashion, transcended human moral categories and can no longer be judged according to any conventional standard—a dangerous power to ascribe to anyone.

Along with this new amorality, Dean embodies a heightened physical intensity that transparently and immediately reflects his emotional state. "Fury spat out of his eyes when he told of things he hated; great glows of joy replaced this when he suddenly got happy; every muscle twitched to live and go" (114). This eccentricity and hyperkinetic energy are depicted in Sal's breathless description:

> He had become absolutely mad in his movements; he seemed to be doing everything at the same time. It was a shaking of the head, up and down, sideways; jerky, vigorous hands; quick walking, sitting, crossing the legs, uncrossing, getting up, rubbing the hands, rubbing his fly, hitching his pants, looking up and saying "Am," and sudden slitting of the eyes to see everywhere; and all the time he was grabbing me by the ribs and talking, talking.
> (114)

Sal, who has been living quietly—attending school and working on the novel Dean has already interrupted once—is again irresistibly swept up. Dean's appetite for life is evident quite literally as he eats a sandwich while dancing "to a wild bop record I had just bought called 'The Hunt,' with Dexter Gordon and Wardell Gray blowing their tops before a screaming audience that gave the record fantastic frenzied volume" (113).

This reference provides a marked contrast to the tedious family "celebration" and brings together a number of the important subcultural images already presented. Ross Russell recorded these sessions in

July 1947 and his liner notes—echoing Sal's discussion of bop in Chicago and his stay with Terry in Los Angeles—suggest an energy and joy that seemed no longer available to white America. "In the war years the Afro-American population of L.A. doubled, tripled, quadrupled," and soon there "were dance halls and music bars, restaurants and bordellos and gambling joints."[1] Central Avenue, where Sal and Terry wandered, had "a lotus land ambiance," writes Russell. Crucial to the function bebop plays in *On the Road* is its distance from the commercial culture of "Paper America." At first, bop records were scarce: "You could find them at a shoe shine stand run by a man called Moose the Mooch" whose sources were the Pullman porters bringing them from Chicago. A "roving dealer called 'Bebop', a messianic advocate of the new music," was another supplier, and he "operated with a portable playback ... in cafeterias or on the sidewalks." Gordon and Gray were part of the jazz scene, and *The Hunt,* a record that is played again during the long party scene (127), was recorded on portable disc cutters during a performance at the Elk's Club. According to Russell, this example demonstrates a kind of musical experience that no longer exists: a live bop jam session captured on vinyl that he describes as "spontaneous combustion," a phrase that answers Sal's "burn, burn, burn like fabulous yellow Roman candles" (8). Russell notes that this combustive scene, while bright, did not burn long. By 1950, like much of the America whose disappearance saddens Sal, this California scene was over.

African American culture seemed, to writers such as Kerouac or Mailer, to preserve something of great value that was vanishing from white America, and this enthusiasm for bop epitomized one, but not the only, aspect of this Beat response to America's segregated racial system. On the same page that refers to *The Hunt,* Dean slows the car to pass "a mule wagon; in it sat an old Negro plodding along" (113). Dean's excitement is immediate and reflects a racial fascination:

> "Yes!" yelled Dean. "Yes! Dig him! Now consider his soul—stop awhile and consider." And he slowed down the car for all of us to turn and look at the old jazzbo moaning along. "Oh yes, dig him sweet; now there's thoughts in that mind that I would give my

last arm to know; to climb in there and find out just what he's poor-ass pondering about this year's turnip greens and ham." (113)

This "moaning" foreshadows one of Sal's moments of insight: "*Go moan for man*," he is told one night by "a tall old man with flowing white hair" (306). And one of Kerouac's best-known recorded readings includes God's instruction to "Go moan," recorded with Steve Allen on piano.[2] For Kerouac, the blues moan, a product of African American experience, indicated a legitimate, direct, and honest response to the human condition.

As in Sal's earlier identification with the "old Negro cotton picker" (97), there is a peculiar mixture of admiration and condescension in this passage, of real interest and of investment in the racial stereotypes that obstruct the possibility of knowledge. This admiration is reserved for someone who appears to live outside modern middle America, whose preservation of an earlier way of life ensures a quality of experience increasingly unavailable in modern America. In a 1949 journal entry, Kerouac wrote that the "future of America lies in the Negro.... It is the simplicity and raw strength, rising out of the American ground, that will save us" ("On the Road Again," 54). This faith is radically conservative, however, predicated as it is on a belief in the innate simplicity of African Americans and on the condition of racist exclusion eventually challenged by the Civil Rights movement. As Podhoretz wrote, "I doubt if a more idyllic picture of Negro life has been painted since certain Southern ideologues tried to convince the world that things were just fine as fine could be for the slaves on the old plantation" (Podhoretz, 311). Dean's inquiring gaze out the car window at this man echoes the previous image of him driving across America staring out like a monk into a manuscript, yet the commitment of these young whites to reading that African American text is thrown seriously into question by their spectatorial attitude. No words are exchanged as they gaze briefly out the car window, as though this farmer were an exhibit in a museum, then drive off, with Dean "suddenly jumping the car back to seventy and hunching over the wheel" (114).

Under Dean's influence once again, Sal soon takes off "at dark" (115) on another frenzied journey. Unlike Sal's highly planned first trip, this journey arises from "a completely meaningless set of circumstances" and Sal goes for "no reason" (116). "Whither goest thou, America, in thy shiny car in the night?" Carlo Marx inquires later on (119), placing the group and its quest in the context of American modernity—a culture possessing the means to create technological marvels but lacking direction. "We sat and didn't know what to say; there was nothing to talk about any more. The only thing to do was go" (119). What follows is a confusing transitional period, spent mostly in New York, as they prepare for another cross-continental drive, the conversations and events conveying the swirling energy and restless exploration of the developing Beat subculture.

There is a thematic consistency in this section in the set of recurrent concerns as they push against the limits of modernity. Dean's curiosity about the African American farmer is echoed in Carlo's prophetic tone and the "fellahin" aura of his recent visit to Dakar, where "wearing a beard, he had wandered the back streets with little children who led him to a witch doctor who told him his fortune. He had snapshots of crazy streets with grass huts, the hip back-end of Dakar" (118–19). Dean's subsequent manic argument, less anthropological and more philosophical, is equally opposed to the Western rationalism that has been the cornerstone of modernity. "Everything since the Greeks has been predicated wrong. You can't make it with geometry and geometrical systems of thinking" (120). With reference to theology and to Nietzsche's critique of philosophy and rationalism, Dean points toward the variety of ways of thinking that have since come to be associated with postmodernism.

The most controversial issue to be explored in this section is male-female relations. The question of whether or not Dean ought to have qualms or scruples about his treatment of women, for example, is considered off and on throughout the novel and at this point Sal and Dean differ. Dean, attempting to transcend conventional morality, wants a relationship based on love and understanding but "with all hassles thrown out" (122)—in other words, with complete freedom to come and go. Unfortunately, the women in his life have difficulty with this. Sal's attitude is shaped by his Catholicism and his aunt, who has asserted that "the world would never find peace until men fell at their women's feet and asked for forgiveness." While his position will shift later, Sal argues here that "we don't understand our women; we blame on them and it's all our fault." Dean, for whom freedom is foremost, wants to move away from notions of fault and blame: "it isn't as simple as that," he argues as they return to find Marylou starving and smoking old cigarette butts from the ashtray. "Peace will come suddenly, we won't understand when it does" (122). The divergence here is almost total: Sal favoring abject and general apology and Dean, increasingly surrounded with the wreckage of his various relationships, wishing to rise above it all. The menu of possible positions considered here is, of course, drastically reduced compared to the revaluation of gender that would begin with the emergence of contemporary feminism a few years later.

Maternal order can be a positive alternative to masculine order in *On the Road.* In a standoff over a speeding ticket between Sal's aunt and police, it is she, "a respectable woman" (122), who emerges as the moral (if not the legal victor) while the police are "flabbergasted." The police represent a repressive modern male order, while matriarchal order appears less a modern than an archaic social form: "the sad, fat brown mother prevailed," writes Sal of Terry's family, "as she always does among the great fellahin peoples of the world" (98). With his increasing sense of "neo-fellahin" identity, Sal (like Kerouac himself) is able to rely on his aunt and her sense of order to prevail in the midst of his own chaotic life. But in this scheme of things, women may play other roles as well. Sal's aunt is a nonsexualized representative of maternal order, but Marylou ("a whore" [172]) appears as a sexualized provoker of male disorder and madness. Not only does she drive Dean into the frenzied state that makes him leave Camille and disappear on his manic binges, she has a strong effect on Sal ("I licked my lips for the luscious blonde" [125]) as well. Her flirting with Sal at a party touches off a domino effect of jealousy and promiscuity that stretches from one party to the next over a period of days to the sound of the same bebop music that opened this section of the novel: *The Hunt* by Dexter Gordon and Wardell Gray. The word *promiscuous* literally refers to mixtures and disorder, and Sal's response is apt: "Everything was being mixed up, and all was falling" (125).

The division of women—by men—into asexual mothers and sexual whores has, of course, a long history and Kerouac's biography demonstrates that he was never able to resolve this opposition. Sal fantasizes a resolution, just as Kerouac himself often did, only a few pages before: "I want to marry a girl . . . so I can rest my soul with her till we both get old. This can't go on all the time—all this franticness and jumping around" (116). As Dean reminds him, however, Sal has been indulging in this dream for years without finding a woman who embodies for him both sexuality and order—and indeed it proved impossible for Kerouac, whose dependence on his mother gradually overwhelmed him. For all his fantasies of romantic love and declarations of attachment, however, Sal never approaches such a situation. He knows his relationships with Terry and Lucille will not last. Still, this intermediate category of women does exist in *On the Road*— women such as Camille and Galatea who can be defined neither as mothers nor as whores and who appear to desire more or less stable heterosexual relationships. It is precisely with these women that tension develops as the men, particularly Dean, maintain other agendas. This discussion of women ends in asexual domestic order as Sal's aunt buys groceries and cooks "a tremendous breakfast" (122).

The next chapter finds Ed Dunkel thinking about women. His thoughts mingle images of a woman who gave him food on a cold Chicago night, his dead mother, and his wife Galatea whom they ditched on the way east (123). As the "snow whirled outside," Ed appears somewhat lost and vulnerable: "He had no direction," comments Sal, and his growing love for Galatea promises to provide some. Given the detailed discussion of gender relations in the section, it is fitting that the frenzied stay in New York ends and the road adventure begins with a call from Bull Lee demanding that they deal with Galatea, Ed's abandoned wife who has sought refuge with him in Louisiana. While Ed wants to rejoin her now, he will disappear again later in the narrative. Women are presented repeatedly as the providers of warmth, shelter, and direction for wandering men, but this has a negative side in that it decreases male autonomy, an issue considered crucial in America at the time. As Ehrenreich has observed, it was thought by many that men were being emasculated by the domestic power of women (wives and mothers) combined with the conformist corporate structures that were increasingly the norm for middle-class American workers (Ehrenreich, 29–41). The problem of gender is crucial to *On the Road,* although—as Ehrenreich points out—it refers to a crisis in masculinity predating the crisis in femininity that erupted in the 1960s and changed the terms of the gender debate almost beyond recognition.

Sexuality and order seem inimical forces, and sexuality—as Dean's behavior demonstrates—can take on a destructive aura. Sal's vision of the Shrouded Traveler, another in the series of prophetic or apocalyptic figures, evidently represents death, but Sal's explanation suggests sexuality as well as death. "The one thing that we yearn for in our living days, that makes us sigh and groan and undergo sweet nauseas of all kinds, is the remembrance of some lost bliss that was probably experienced in the womb and can only be reproduced (though we hate to admit it) in death. But who wants to die?" (124). Sexuality, evidently a sign of life in Dean, is for Sal simultaneously a desire for the womb and for death. Disorder is manifested as Dean announces his desire to watch Sal and Marylou have sex. Although Marylou is willing, Sal is unable and they agree to try again in California. Once there, however, disorder continues to rule and Sal is abandoned first by Dean and then by Marylou, precipitating his brief mental breakdown moment of vision. Sal describes these explorations as "a great forum we were having" (132), although this neutral term inadequately suggests the chaos into which they descend: "the confusion of jam on the floor, pants, dresses thrown around, cigarette butts, dirty dishes, open books.... Marylou was black and blue from a fight with Dean about something; his face was scratched" (132–33).

However difficult, confusing, and even violent the exploration, the attempt to find what lies in the space beyond conventional moral qualms continues: "Every day the world groaned to turn and we were making our appalling studies of the night" (132–33), writes Sal, continuing the metaphor introduced in reference to Dean and the wintry manuscript he studied. As the long party scene reaches its feverish crescendo, Sal, Dean, and the "ragged gang" encounter Rollo Greb, a man whose manic energy rivals Dean's. Dean is so impressed that "with head bowed," he states his admiration to an uncomprehending Sal: "Man, he's the end! You see, if you go like him all the time you'll finally get it." When Sal replies with a question ("Get what?"), Dean responds, "IT! IT!" (127). This passage picks up the discussion that Sal had with Dean and Carlo in Denver, when Sal had insisted "That the last thing is what you can't get.... Nobody can get to the last thing. We keep on living in hopes of catching it once and for all" (48). Dean has grown more intense in the interim, now arguing that it is indeed possible to catch "IT" if one moves fast enough and, like the "wild, ecstatic" Greb, never gets "hung-up" (127). The frenetic atmosphere—the excitement, the music, the marijuana—leads Sal yet again to the brink of revelation. "It made me think that everything was about to arrive—the moment when you know all and everything is decided forever" (129). As usual with Sal's intimations of Truth, however, revelation is deferred and finality is postponed. The cure for confusion seems not to be order but movement, not knowledge but speed: "we were leaving confusion and nonsense behind and performing our one and noble function of the time, *move*. And we moved!" (133–34).

As he drives, Dean continues to propound his new philosophy. The first tenet is clear: move. And he sums up the second simply: "there's no need in the world to worry." His case rests largely on his own persuasive example: "you know that I'm hotrock capable of everything at the same time and I have unlimited energy" (134). Dean's solution to the problem of time is to master it, to refuse its unilinearity, to do everything at the same time and thus negate the limits of time. The antithesis of this individuality and velocity has been glimpsed in the police presence that occasionally obstructs momentum. The repressive power of the state gains visibility on Truman's inauguration day as they pass through Washington with its military spectacles. "Great displays of war might were lined along Pennsylvania Avenue as we rolled by.... all kinds of war material that looked murderous in the snowy grass" (135). Foreshadowing the incomprehension of antiwar protesters years later, Dean "kept shaking his head in awe. 'What are these people up to?' " This bewilderment at the symbols of the central power structure of America indicates the degree to which these bohemian adventurers have become alienated from mainstream society and its values. Their only response to official America is suggested in Dean's earlier parodic reading of the newspaper: "Ah, our holy American slopjaws in Washington are planning fur-ther [*sic*] inconveniences—ah-hem!—aw—hup! hup!" (115).

This point is brought home even more clearly in the next paragraph as they encounter other agents of the state. Dean's lack of synchronization with the rules is clear as he makes a triple pass driving the wrong way "in the fourth lane in a four-lane highway"—and does so past a police officer who pulls the car over. It may be that their "one and noble function of the time" is to move, but "the cop took after us with his siren whining. We were stopped" (135). These events continue the extended discussion of the police and social control begun in the Mill City episode. This time Dean's driving is only the beginning; as soon becomes clear, the police are suspicious as well of the whole arrangement, sensing rightly that these people do not fit in. The pretext for stopping them is speeding, but the questioning soon turns to their unorthodox relationships. After threats and a fine, they are able to leave, but the encounter reminds Sal of the "cop-soul," a description anticipating Michel Foucault's analysis of the surveillance mentality that is a central feature of modern society. The power mechanism was in many ways more intrusive in Cold War America when the state not only determined the laws and their enforcement but also aggressively enforced unwritten codes of normality: "The American police are involved in psychological warfare against those Americans who don't frighten them with imposing papers and threats," Sal declares. "It's a Victorian police force; it peers out of musty windows and wants to inquire about everything, and can make crimes if the crimes don't exist to its satisfaction" (136). This oppressive order has created an America that appears unremittingly grim to Sal, far removed from the "wild selfbelieving" American spirit whose remnants Kerouac is seeking: "the long, bleak street with the railroad track running down the middle and the sad, sullen Southerners loping in front of hardware stores and five-and-tens" (137). The police men-

tality exists as a limit to Dean's speed but also to their ability to continue challenging convention through their "appalling" but com-
pelling "studies of the night" (132–33).

The hitchhiker they pick up after leaving the police, "a ragged,
bespectacled mad type" named Hyman Solomon, is reading a book he
has found by the roadside, reading with great attention "as though he
had found the real Torah where it belonged, in the wilderness" (137).
The wilderness—geographical or psychological, natural or urban—
remains the real source of understanding, but police presence typically
prevents access to it. Such separations and barriers cannot succeed
though, according to Dean, who notes the coincidence of this strange
biblical character and the return through Testament, the biblically
named town where this section began: "all things [are] tied together
all over like rain connecting everybody the world over by chain
touch" (138). This rainy night image—echoing the earlier reference to
"the myth of the rainy night" (128) and anticipating the full discussion
just ahead—rekindles the excitement that had preceded the police
intervention; indeed for Sal, it returns to the very beginning of the
book and the quest motif that started it all off: "He and I suddenly
saw the whole country like an oyster for us to open; and the pearl was
there, the pearl was there" (138).

They arrive in New Orleans to the strains of jazz on the car radio
as once again their image of African American culture provides a
model: "a momentous mad thing began on the radio; it was the
Chicken Jazz'n Gumbo disk-jockey show from New Orleans, all mad
jazz records, colored records, with the disk-jockey saying, 'Don't
worry 'bout *nothing!*' " (140). This advice repeats exactly Dean's
approach to worry, and moments later the scene is completed with the
image of "Negroes ... working in the hot afternoon, stoking the ferry
furnaces that burned red" (141), and women who make Dean point
and shout. Like Sal's experience with the field workers or the recent
encounter with the farmer, African American "fellahin" life provides
them with a sense of possibility otherwise denied. Here, the excitement moves Dean to his characteristic rapture; sweating in response to
the heat of the day, of the furnaces, and of sexual desire, he exclaims
"Ah! God! Life!" (140).

The stay with Bull Lee and Jane presents another kind of eccentric possibility. The images Sal provides of them are important, as the models for these characters—William S. Burroughs and Joan Vollmer Adams Burroughs—were central to the development of Beat culture. Before she moved south with Burroughs, in fact, Joan had the New York apartment that was the original hub for the Beat group. According to Nicosia, Joan "was a brilliant young Barnard graduate ... a beautiful woman whose contempt for flattery developed into a protective gloss of sophistication and cynicism"(Nicosia, 110). These qualities suited her for marriage with Burroughs, himself a brilliant drug addict whose life remains legendary in the annals of Beat culture. Kerouac provides some details in his brief sketch of Lee—his international adventures with aristocrats and derelicts, his experience as a serious student and as a felon—but most important for Sal is his role as educator: "he was a teacher, and ... he had every right to teach because he spent all his time learning" (143). For Kerouac and Ginsberg, William Burroughs's influence stretched back to the early formative days of the Beats in New York when, as students at Columbia University, they had been challenged by the radical squalor of his personal life—self-induced poverty, drugs, petty crime, homosexuality—and by his strengths as an uncompromising intellectual.

Like Sal, Lee has "a sentimental streak about the old days in America ... [when] the country was wild and brawling and free, with abundance and any kind of freedom for everyone. His chief hate was Washington bureaucracy; second to that liberals; then cops" (144–45). Lee shares none of Sal's soft-edged romantic nostalgia, however, and his tone is far more abrasive. His disappointment with modern America is articulated in his discussion of the ideal bar and its disappearance. Once bars were for men, he argues,

> all there was was a long counter, brass rails, spittoons, player piano for music, a few mirrors, and barrels of whiskey at ten cents a shot together with barrels of beer at five cents a shot. Now all you get is chromium, drunken women, fags, hostile bartenders, anxious owners who hover around the door worried about their leather seats and the law. (146–47)

Lee's running commentary on the decline of America covers much territory and has something to offend many people: unions, plastic, planned obsolescence, bars, construction materials, toothpaste, bureaucracy, orgone accumulation, and the misguided direction of modern science all come into Lee's sights. While Lee and Dean both exercise a major influence on Sal, they otherwise have little in common—in real life, Cassady and Burroughs did not get along especially well either. Both socially marginal and eccentric, their contrasting sensibilities are demonstrated on the ferry trip that night: while Lee stays in the car convinced of his pessimistic position, Dean—hungry for experience—goes outside, leaning over the rail, looking out at the night, at the river and the ships in the fog, and at the "Negroes [who] plied the shovel and sang" (147).

Sal's vision of the river finally takes up the myth of the rainy night. Kerouac was constantly in the process of creating a mythology out of whatever raw materials he could—his childhood, his friends' childhoods, their exploits during this formative Beat period, but also—as we have seen in some of his descriptions of the geography of America—out of the land itself. The myth of the rainy night was an important notion for him, and it even appears as the subtitle to an early version of *Doctor Sax*. When they enter New Orleans, Sal looks out at the Mississippi, "the great brown father of waters rolling down from mid-America like the torrent of broken souls," carrying logs and mud and "things that had drowned" all the way from the river's source "where the secret began in ice" (141). In a postcard to Ginsberg written from Montana not long after the actual visit that *On the Road* narrates, Kerouac explains his fascination with the river:

> Here I am at the sources of the rainy night, where the Missouri River starts ... to roll in the tidal midland night down to Algiers [Louisiana] bearing Montana logs past the house where Old Bill Lee sits. The rainy night is a river (NO LAKE). The rain is the sea coming back—and waters so fluid flow in their appointed serene beds with satisfaction & eternity (like men really do) to the Gulf of the Night." (*Letters,* 183)

This vision of the endless transformational cycle of water rising from the sea, becoming rain that falls to flow in rivers back to the sea, provided Kerouac with a metaphor for human life, for history, for the endless cycle of birth and death. At this moment, the process appears so natural and serene that he can accept calmly his place in it all— including his mortality. The flood, an inseparable aspect of Kerouac's rainy night, is a powerful reminder of the transitory nature of life, its continual flow and transformation until the final transformation in "the Gulf of the Night," which is itself a new beginning. Like Dean's recent insight into the unifying nature of rain, Sal's vision is all-encompassing: "as the river poured down from mid-America by starlight I knew, I knew like mad that everything I had ever known and would ever know was One" (147).

Crossing the Mississippi once again as they head west, Sal meditates a final time on the brown river's symbolic meaning. The crossing occurs at Port Allen, where we "suddenly saw the great black body below a bridge and crossed eternity again." Like the Hudson River on his first attempt to hitchhike west, this river is "all rain and roses in a misty pinpoint darkness":

> What is the Mississippi River?—a washed clod in that rainy night, a soft plopping from drooping Missouri banks, a dissolving, a riding of the tide down the eternal waterbed, a contribution to brown foams, a voyaging past endless vales and trees and levees, down along, down along, by Memphis, Greenville, Eudora, Vicksburg, Natchez, Port Allen, and Port Orleans and Port of the Deltas, by Potash, Venice, and the Night's Great Gulf, and out. (156)

With the emergence into this Great Gulf of Night, the voyage of the Mississippi from its secret sources is completed in oblivion, only to begin again with the rainy night. As though to underscore the loss of such an elevating and unifying vision in American modernity, Kerouac moves from the (timeless) sublime to the (modern) ridiculous as this passage is immediately followed by a description of billboard advertisements for paint.

This vision of nature and nation is quite literally blocked, however, when he tries to get to the river to continue his thoughts. "I wanted to sit on the muddy bank and dig the Mississippi River; instead of that I had to look at it with my nose against a wire fence. When you start separating the people from their rivers, what have you got? 'Bureaucracy!' says Old Bull; he sits with Kafka on his lap.... And the Montana log rolls by in the big black river of the night" (148). The problem here concerns the intrusion of modern rules and constraints, exemplified both by the chain link fence—an icon of modernity due to its presence in industrial zones and in concentration camps—and by the reference to Kafka, a great writer whose narratives illuminate peculiarly modern forms of anxiety, despair, and humor like no other. At this point then, the redemptive and unified vision of America inspired by the river and its apparently timeless connections to an original purity is hopelessly obstructed by modernity's divisive grids. But in the end, modernity may not be able to contain the flow: one of Kerouac's enduring youthful memories was of the 1936 Lowell flood which irreparably harmed his father's business and the family's livelihood. It is interesting to note that in *Doctor Sax*, Kerouac's fictionalized version of that flood ends with a cautionary note about what can happen to "civilization when it gets caught with its pants down from a source it long lost contact with." And he is clear about whose pants were down: "City Hall golf politicians and clerks... complained that the river had drowned all the fairways and tees, these knickers types were disgruntled by natural phenomena."[3]

This sense of the transitory also lies behind the novel's repeated wistful departures. As they drive away, Sal asks one of the most poignant questions in this narrative of inexplicable arrivals and arbitrary departures: "What is that feeling when you're driving away from people and they recede on the plain till you see their specks dispersing?—it's the too-huge world vaulting us, and it's goodby. But we lean forward to the next crazy venture beneath the skies" (156). Like the myth of the rainy night or Spengler's theory of the rise and fall of empires, time and experience flow away, impossible to grasp, a continuous process of loss and new beginning experienced without the consolation of an overarching explanatory mythology to make it all cohere and resist the apparent insignificance of human action. This instability may lead to a feeling of futility or meaninglessness but also to a liberation from the conventional rules that attempt to lend structure and importance to human "specks" and their actions in the "too-huge world."

This form of separation anxiety recurs a number of times. In Tucson, after a visit with Hal Hingham, Sal writes, "It was sad to see his tall figure receding in the dark as we drove away, just like other figures in New York and New Orleans: they stand uncertainly underneath immense skies, and everything about them is drowned.... But this foolish gang was bending forward" (166–67). Kerouac's use of the term "drowned" connects it to the rainy night and a flow of time beyond human comprehension. Their only option is to keep going ("bending forward") without any clear sense of where the pearl might be found. This phenomenon recurs, and the metaphor continues to involve water and night: leaving Ed Wall's house, for example, Sal "turned to watch the kitchen light recede in the sea of night. Then I leaned ahead" (229). This describes a spatial loss but more importantly a temporal loss, as he bends forward into the future without ever having grasped the present or the past. Kerouac's nickname—Memory Babe—suggests his phenomenal memory but also his phenomenal need to remember in order to hold events back from some vanishing point beyond which they would be lost and unredeemed to significance. Ginsberg once recalled that he and Kerouac shared an understanding that "you were only in your own one place very briefly, in a sense ghosts because so transient, everybody lost in a dream world of their own making. Really a kind of farewell dream." This feeling of temporal as well as geographical transience was, Ginsberg claims, crucial: "We talked about that a lot and that really was the basis of the Beat Generation, the poignant kewpee doll dearness of personages vanishing in time" (Miles, 69).

Dean wholeheartedly resists resignation, attempting instead a total recall of the past in order to keep it from disappearing. "Man, if my memory could only serve me right the way my mind works I could tell you every detail of the things we did" (158). A few pages later, Dean emotionally describes his time in reform school (162), and as they arrive in Bakersfield, it seems crucial for him not only to remember but also to tell every detail. In Kerouac's work, the past is not safe unless secured in narrative.

> Dean wanted to tell me everything he knew about Bakersfield as
> we reached the city limits. He showed me rooming houses where
> he'd stayed, railroad hotels, poolhalls, diners, sidings where he
> jumped off the engine for grapes, Chinese restaurants where he
> ate, park benches where he met girls, and certain places where
> he'd done nothing but sit and wait around.... He remembered
> all—every pinochle game, every woman, every sad night. (168)

Without any sense of purpose beyond movement, speed, and kicks,
there is no way to redeem the past from oblivion other than to
remember every detail. For years, Cassady read Marcel Proust's *A la
Recherche du Temps Perdu* (Clarke, 105). The standard English translation is "The Remembrance of Things Past," an apt borrowing from
Shakespeare's Sonnet 30—but in Cassady's case, the literal translation
is also worth noting: "In Search of Lost Time" captures an essence of
his ongoing struggle with temporality.

The next sections provide glimpses of ways of living outside
modernity's grip. The "great black body" of the Mississippi—a fundamental aspect of Kerouac's attempt to write an American mythology—
is echoed on the next page in another recurring image of black bodies
which Kerouac found as irresistible here in the rural deep South as he
had in Harlem or the New Orleans waterfront: "Man, do you imagine
what it would be like if we found a jazzjoint in these swamps, with
great big black fellas moanin guitar blues and drinking snakejuice and
makin signs at us?" (157). A clear example, for Kerouac, of people
who managed to live outside this modern America, African Americans
appear not so much as real people but as allegorical symbols of the
"fellahin" ability to survive and maintain a vital culture in adverse
conditions. Unlike the white culture he found so shallow, these people
appeared to him to maintain contact with meaningful truths while living on the margins of a social structure that seemed bent on the eradi-
cation of such awareness while playing out its historical drama of cultural decline. But the swampland remains impenetrable, and here Sal
confronts a limit in his recurrent textual metaphor: "This was a manuscript of the night we couldn't read" (158).

Much more legible is Dean's account of a dissolute stay in Texas,
a tale of drugs, promiscuous sex, and voyages into the "spade part of

town" (158). This short flashback of Dean's evinces an astonishing amorality. In the early postwar era, discussion of drugs and sexuality had far more shock value than in the present when such behavior is more familiar, but even so it is difficult to maintain sympathy. When Hassel disappeared looking for drugs, Dean brought a "dumb girl" ("out of her mind . . . her idiot mind") back to the room for sex, while Bull Lee plied a boy with alcohol and Marx took heroin. This account would have appalled the average reader at that time, but it is recounted without moral comment. While it was precisely such moments as these that opened the novel to charges of amorality from its attackers, its defenders saw this problem as a central theme of *On the Road*. The "appalling studies of the night," being conducted along the lines of the Dostoyevsky novels they were influenced by, have suspended conventional moral categories in order to test their coherence. As is the case in Dostoyevsky's *The Possessed*, for example, unless some justification for moral "qualms" can be established, there is nothing to stand against this behavior.

In Houston, Sal, Dean, and Marylou encounter another classic male figure of postwar alienation—this one typically white rather than black—and one that would attain the status of a cultural icon through mass media representations such as *The Wild One* or *Easy Rider* years later. "In the empty Houston streets of four o'clock in the morning a motorcycle kid suddenly roared through, all bespangled and bedecked with glittering buttons, visor, slick black jacket, a Texas poet of the night, girl gripped on his back like a papoose, hair flying, onward-going" (159). This black-clad young man appears to have not only read "the manuscript of the night" but also inscribed it with his own poetic message and image. As the Beat Generation itself would, the motorcycle-jacketed youth became entrenched in the popular imagination of the time along with juvenile delinquents, nonconformists, Elvis and James Dean, as quintessential male symptoms of postwar social dysfunction and resistance. These two images of American rebellion—the Beat and the biker—almost merged, in fact, when the possibility arose that Marlon Brando, Johnny in *The Wild One*, would play the part of Dean in a movie version of *On the Road* (Nicosia, 559).

The Second Journey

As they move farther west, Dean's behavior becomes increasingly extreme, and the journey spirals into chaos. Sal even admits at one point that he no longer knows what Dean is talking about (161). Passing drivers are shocked to see Dean, Marylou, and Sal naked and smeared with cold cream as they cross Texas. Leaving the car to explore an Indian ruin, Sal and Marylou put on overcoats but Dean goes out "stark naked" to the disbelieving stares of passing tourists (161–62). After more misadventures, more hitchhikers, more money troubles, and more petty theft of food, gas, and cigarettes, they arrive. But despite their attempt to challenge and clarify morality and conventionality through a strategic transgression of some basic rules of behavior in their pursuit of "kicks," no sense of finality is achieved. This voyage ends with no more sense of accomplishment than arrival itself, no more point than that the road goes no farther: "Wow! Made it! Just enough gas! Give me water! No more land! We can't go any further 'cause there ain't no more land!" (170). And at this point, Dean, whose energy had propelled them, abandons them to their own insufficient devices as he moves on to another phase of his life.

Deprived of Dean's momentum and feeling betrayed, Sal and Marylou collapse into sadness and disorientation. In another of the recurring references to rags and raggedness, Sal laments that "We wandered around, carrying our bundles of rags" in a California that is anything but a land of dreams. The upbeat experience of the streets Sal enjoyed with Terry is now reversed, and "Everybody looked like a broken-down movie extra, a withered starlet; disenchanted stunt-men, midget auto-racers, poignant California characters with their end-of-the-continent sadness" (170). Sal stays in San Francisco for one week, and it is in this setting that he has "the beatest time of my life" (171). Without money, food, or shelter, Sal and Marylou find themselves in the hotel room of a nightclub singer, heating a can of beans on an iron supported by a coat hanger, visiting drunken sailors who give them whiskey, and, after a couple of days, observes Sal, "I was out of my mind with hunger and bitterness" (172). The descent is complete when Marylou—like Dean—abandons Sal to go with "a greasy old man with a roll" of money. Sal, as usual, is quick to condemn her for this: "I saw what a whore she was" (172), he comments, echoing

Dean's words (5–6). The downward spiral that began with Dean's Christmastime arrival leaves Sal at one of his life's lowest points: "Now," writes Sal, "I had nobody, nothing."

This state of exhaustion and hunger propels him to a visionary state, "delirious" and "frozen with ecstasy" (172). Abandoned first by Marylou, whom he classifies as a "whore," he then has a vision of rejection by a mother figure as well, and this vision propels him to a new experience of temporality and identity, articulated in a rhetorical style unlike any in the novel so far:

> I had reached the point of ecstasy that I always wanted to reach, which was the complete step across chronological time into timeless shadows, and wonderment in the bleakness of the mortal realm, and the sensation of death kicking at my heels to move on, with a phantom dogging its own heels, and myself hurrying to a plank where all the angels dove off and flew into the holy void of uncreated emptiness, the potent and inconceivable radiancies shining in the bright Mind Essence, innumerable lotuslands falling open in the magic mothswarm of heaven. (173)

This moment is another—the most dramatic thus far—in the series of revelatory moments when Sal appears to grasp the truth he has searched for. It is a truth that has to do with the fluidity—not stability or permanence—of identity, memory, truth, and knowledge. In this, it resembles the fluidity basic to the myth of the rainy night, even in its employment of water metaphors.

> I realized that I had died and been reborn numberless times but just didn't remember especially because the transitions from life to death and back to life are so ghostly easy, a magical action for naught, like falling asleep and waking up again a million times, the utter casualness and deep ignorance of it. I realized that it was only because of the stability of the intrinsic Mind that these ripples of birth and death took place, like the action of wind upon a sheet of pure, serene, mirror-like water. (173)

This passage has relevance not only for Sal's understanding of mortality and reincarnation, but also for the structure of identity that it conveys. Robert Creeley has remarked that Kerouac "worked the pronoun 'I' so variously that its use now provokes of necessity some real question," and the stability of the self is seriously undermined here.[4] As we have seen, Sal's sense of personal identity is extremely changeable, moving from hobo to prophet to Hollywood screenwriter to dutiful son to debauched youth to saint and so on. Continuously reborn in a variety of identities, Sal is always eager to specify the most recent as the final real and true one. But this process is "a magical action for naught" because nothing lasts, and the wind that stirs the ripples on the surface of his identity soon ceases or shifts, and world and self are changed once again. "I thought I was going to die the very next moment," he declares, searching again for some finality, some closure, but it once again eludes him. Instead, he returns to life and desire again, looking for good-sized cigarette butts on the sidewalk as he wanders the city dreaming of food. "I was too young to know what had happened," Sal comments in retrospect (173), adding yet another level of instability with this suggestion that his identity and understanding of the world have shifted once again in subsequent years.

If the whole process of the ceaseless elaboration and collapse of identity appears to be "a magical action for naught" rather than the finding of the pearl, then it is not inappropriate that the Dean Moriarty he next encounters is another Dean than the one who had traveled with him so recently. Dean too is constantly shifting, one moment utterly committed to Sal and "kicks," the next minute dumping him in San Francisco without a cent. First a free-spirited thrill-seeker, now he returns as a married man, a devoted husband and father, trying to provide for his family as a door-to-door salesman. Still, flashes of the other Dean rekindle Sal's faith: "One morning he stood naked, looking at all San Francisco out the window as the sun came up. He looked like someday he'd be the pagan mayor of San Francisco" (175). Dean's skills as a con man and the presence of women on his door-to-door route cannot hold his interest long though, and he soon hands in his kitchen appliances. "In a dead silence the salesman gathered up his sad pots and left. I was sick and tired of everything and so was Dean" (175). It is to be expected though that, yet again, this deadness will be the site of some new life.

This mood of desolation is broken, as is often the case, with a night out—this time in the San Francisco jazz scene in an atmosphere of desperate pleasures: "It was the end of the continent; they didn't give a damn" (177). Here they see legendary musician Slim Gaillard, a "Negro with big sad eyes" (175), whose sadness was more than mediated by the zany humor of his music and performance style. Gaillard, who made up half the duo Slim and Slam (with Slam Stewart) and who later played with Dizzy Gillespie, Charlie Parker, and Harry "The Hipster" Gibson, combined a virtuoso musical style with unique and eccentric vocals. The linguistic inventiveness that led to lyrics such as "Flat Foot Floogie with a Floy Floy" and "Yip Roc Heresy" came from his interest in languages, and while he may not have known "innumerable languages," as Sal claims, he borrows from them the sounds that make up "Vout," his own language of nonsense syllables. "To Slim Gaillard the whole world was just one big orooni," reflects Sal (177), appreciative of this attempt to transcend the sadness and uniformity of modern America through irony, madcap humor, and weirdness in combination with hot jazz.

Sal decides to head east, but not before one last wild night out "hitting the Negro jazz shacks" with Dean and Marylou (178). This is one of the few points at which racial tension interrupts their pursuit of "kicks" across racial lines, a night that concludes with a sense of exhaustion at the end of the continent: "It was the end; I wanted to get out" (178). A dispirited group as they part company, Sal even refuses to share his food with Dean and Marylou, and no one cares whether or not they ever meet up again. Another burst of hipster energy has propelled them through a frantic and intense period, but only to end in desolate exhaustion—a pattern like the myth of the rainy night, like Spengler's rise and fall of empires, and like Sal's assumption of identities.

7

The Third Journey

Part 3 begins with a sense of narrative disjunction. Sal's stay in the East is entirely omitted from the narrative, and the next chapter opens in the spring of 1949 when Sal goes to settle down in a new life and a new self in Denver. "I saw myself in Middle America, a patriarch" (179), he writes, although it is unclear how such an unlikely identity ever occurred to him at all. The imaginary identity he has projected this time collapses almost immediately, however. Instead of the substantial worldly presence he has anticipated, none of his old friends can be found, and he feels reduced to insignificance: "I felt like a speck on the surface of the sad red earth" (180). Feeling lost, he wanders Denver looking for direction.

This moment of searching provides one of the novel's most lyrical and most frequently criticized episodes. Without a white patriarchal model to sustain him, he again looks beyond whiteness, and this section draws together the images of African America the novel has presented thus far. "At lilac evening I walked with every muscle aching among the lights of 27th and Welton in the Denver colored section, wishing I were a Negro, feeling that the best the white world had offered was not enough ecstasy for me, not enough life, joy, kicks, darkness, music, not enough night" (180). Sal's hope centers on the energy that, he believes, is still extant outside the enervated cultural mainstream. Protected from modernity's erosion of individuality and creativity, those excluded groups appear as the heirs of America's promise of freedom far more than the white middle classes who have lost their joy in living as they surrounded themselves with bureaucracy and police. At a time when (pre-Civil Rights) America maintained explicitly racist political and cultural divisions, it is peculiar to see the victims of that political oppression cast as the true heirs of American freedom. Even as African Americans were about to mount their most determined and successful campaign to combat the systemic racism excluding them from mainstream America, Sal attributes freedom and happiness to them precisely on the basis of the exclusion.

"Passing" was a well-known phenomenon but was generally a one-way street on which light-skinned African Americans could merge themselves into white America by denying their racial and cultural ancestry. The advantages of passing in a racist system that denied upward mobility to African Americans were obvious. Sal's desire to be "a Negro" is a very different matter since he is seeking downward mobility in the belief that life is fuller outside the confines of materialistic modern white America. Denver's "colored section," he feels, provides both light and darkness, heat and mystery, in contrast to the bland experience of white America.

> I stopped at a little shack where a man sold hot red chili in paper containers; I bought some and ate it, strolling in the dark mysterious streets. I wished I were a Denver Mexican, or even a poor overworked Jap, anything but what I was so drearily, a "white man" disillusioned. All my life I'd had white ambitions; that was why I'd abandoned a good woman like Terry in the San Joaquin Valley. (180)

In Sal's mind now, the "fellahin" alternative to white life represented by Terry, for example, is far more appealing, offering a quality and texture to life that modernity seems to lack: "I passed the dark porches of Mexican and Negro homes; soft voices were there, occasionally the dusky knee of some mysterious sensual gal; and dark faces of the men behind rose arbors. Little children sat like sages in ancient rocking chairs" (180). A moment of misrecognition leaves Sal even more alienated and nostalgic:

> A gang of colored women came by, and one of the young ones detached herself from the motherlike elders and came to me fast—"Hello Joe!"—and suddenly saw it wasn't Joe, and ran back, blushing. I wished I were Joe. I was only myself, Sal Paradise, sad, strolling in this violet dark, this unbearably sweet night, wishing I could change worlds with the happy, true-hearted, ecstatic Negroes of America. (180)

This coincidental case of mistaken identity—the third following two with Terry—puts pressure on Sal's already volatile sense of self, his desire to belong in these "raggedy neighborhoods" (180), his fantasy that identity might be traded or invented almost at will.

While celebrations of diversity and difference are frequent in the novel, here Kerouac goes further. It is not difficult to point out the problems with this passage: Sal's longing tells us little about any other world, and Kerouac's romantic lyricism overlooks almost entirely the real struggles faced by the people he describes. As he gazes at the African American family, he is filled with envy for this "life that knows nothing of disappointment and 'white sorrows' " (181). The suggestion seems to be that African Americans are insulated from disappointment because they are lacking in aspiration, a notion that can be sustained only at a considerable distance from any actually existing African American community. Nor could these fantasies of the placid and joyous "fellahin" have survived exposure to the intense African American literary culture of the time which included Richard Wright, Ann Petry, Chester Himes, and Ralph Ellison, writers whose articulations of disappointment and frustration are, to put it mildly, unmistakable. In light of all this, the passage seems an act of almost willful ignorance. Kenneth Rexroth, a former ally who had taken a dislike to Kerouac, once asserted that Kerouac knew nothing about "jazz and Negroes" (Clarke, 167).

This assertion is unfair: Kerouac had a great appreciation of jazz, and he did know something about African American culture but clearly not enough. He knew that while enduring centuries of racism, African Americans had created a culture of astonishing creativity, vibrancy, and solidarity. Much African American literature testifies to the cultural richness developed in this community, and Kerouac demonstrates a degree of awareness of this that is unusual in a white writer of that time. Still, he is unable to avoid many of the racial stereotypes common to white America, and he evidently had little comprehension of the real conditions in which these cultural forms flourished, the cost of racist exclusion, and the long history of struggle against those conditions.

It is not difficult here to realize the limitations of Sal's naive vision, and ultimately his predicament conceals more than it reveals about "the happy, true-hearted, ecstatic Negroes of America" (180). Kerouac's ethnic others rarely emerge from a romantic pastoral simplicity. In the end, in light of the cultural limits of Kerouac's flight and his eventual retreat to alcohol-fuelled right-wing delirium, one might question whether Kerouac's work does not ultimately do far more to confuse the issues than to clarify them, more to reinforce than to destabilize rigid categories of racial identity. Still, to dismiss this aspect of Kerouac's vision entirely would be as simplistic as to elevate him to the level of saintly and infallible cult hero, which some hagiographic Kerouac studies continue to do.

Contrasting a sandlot baseball game with his own sports experience, Sal is left, once again, with a sense of sadness and loss. "Never in my life as an athlete had I ever permitted myself to perform like this in front of families and girl friends and kids of the neighborhood," (181) he writes. His efforts were geared to "white ambitions" instead of to physical pleasure, the affirmation of the self, and a sense of community. Now, he feels, the chance has slipped away: "always it had been college, big-time, sober-faced; no boyish, human joy like this. Now it was too late." As the entire narrative has pointed out, these "white ambitions" have not provided him with a foundation on which to construct an identity, a reality, and his response to seeing ordinary people apparently secure and content outside the white mainstream is a dissolution of self: "It was the Denver Night; all I did was die.... How I died!" (181). These metaphoric deaths indicate Sal's fragile selfhood, an identity constantly reinvented only to dissolve again under the pressure of circumstances. This death and rebirth is the process he came to understand during his visionary experience in San Francisco, and it possesses the same fluid structure as the myth of the rainy night with its perpetual transformation. For the moment, however, Sal's rapture continues as he describes the game in terms suggesting a utopian vision of heterogeneous but unified American community. "The strange young heroes of all kinds, white, colored, Mexican, pure Indian, were on the field, performing with heart-breaking seriousness.... Near me sat an old Negro who apparently watched the games. Next to him was an old white bum; then a Mexican family, then some girls, some boys—all humanity, the lot" (180–81).

Sal, ironically, feels excluded from this benign community of the excluded, and in response he substitutes another community affiliation to compensate. This is the Beat Generation, "the sordid hipsters of America" (54), and Dean and Marylou, representatives of an excluded "raggedy" white America, are mentioned here as examples. Sal heads back to San Francisco believing that he has finally made a decisive break with the world of "white ambitions" and can begin anew with a new identity and sense of community. His language rings with determination: "I was burning to know...what would happen now, for there was nothing behind me any more, all my bridges were gone and I didn't give a damn about anything at all" (182). This statement echoes Huck Finn's declaration that he will go to hell rather than be compromised, and confirmation comes from above: crossing through the West in the company of pimps, Sal sees "God in the sky in the form of huge gold sunburning clouds above the desert that seemed to point a finger at me and say, 'Pass here and go on, you're on the road to heaven' " (182). These protestations must be taken with a large grain of salt, however, considering that previous moments of similarly inspired vision and decision have not always proved reliable.

As he travels, leaving behind dreams of Middle America and becoming a patriarch, inspiration comes from the eccentric and lost American spirit betrayed in Cheyenne's Wild West Week but preserved in the remnants and reminders scattered along the desert highway "where there were huts with the weatherbeaten signs still flapping in the haunted shrouded desert wind, saying 'Rattlesnake Bill lived here' or 'Broken-mouth Annie holed up here for years' " (182). These are traces of the "raggedy" American spirit Sal is searching for, the "wild selfbelieving" individuality he is trying to affirm in spite of the postwar tendency toward homogeneity and systematization. The "shrouded" wind, a version of death's Shrouded Traveler, has swept them away as living presences, but in keeping with the transformational myth of the rainy night, Sal believes that the "wild selfbelieving" spirit of America will be reborn and that Dean represents the best white male hope Sal knows for the reemergence of this endangered America. When Sal arrives at two A.M., Dean's appearance, unconcealed and unsublimated, is typical: "He came to the door stark naked.... He received the world in the raw" (182).

In the context of Dean's precarious domestic circumstances with Camille and their young daughter, Sal's arrival is "like the coming of the strange most evil angel in the home of the snow-white fleece.... Apparently Dean had been quiet for a few months; now the angel had arrived and he was going mad again" (183). The scene is a tense one. Camille, unintentionally pregnant again, is crying and calling Dean a liar—which, of course, he is despite his willingness to receive "the world in the raw." The car is gone, and with it their money. Dean is out of work, and punching Marylou has left him with a broken thumb. His obsession with Marylou has deepened, now combining sexual, suicidal, and homicidal tendencies. Yet, typically, the problem is presented as Camille's, not Dean's. Sal writes: "It was horrible to hear Camille sobbing so. We couldn't stand it and went out to buy beer." When the sobbing stops and Camille lapses into silence, he surmises that either she has fallen asleep at last or she will spend "the night staring blankly at the dark" (183).

It is possible that Sal's next line—"I had no idea what was really wrong"—is an ironic comment, but it may simply assert Sal's (or Kerouac's) inability to imagine the situation of women of the period, both bohemian and straight. If it seems that chaos is the price of living intensely, of living like a burning roman candle, then Sal accepts that it must be paid, and Dean's domestic catastrophe is further proof that he is exempt from convention and subject to another, more vital set of imperatives. The fact that Sal himself arrives on the scene feeling that all his bridges to straight life are burnt contributes no doubt to his willingness to embrace Dean's actions, however extreme and erratic and whatever the effect on Camille. Despite all this, Dean's tale of madness and woe concludes on an incongruously upbeat note. "I've never felt better and finer and happier with the world" (186), he declares, oddly ascribing this happiness to the joys of domesticity and parenthood. This endorsement is immediately juxtaposed, however, with the announcement that "in the morning Camille threw both of us out."

The discussion of gender continues to build from there and inspires one of Sal's rare and brief attempts to consider things from a female point of view. Returning from work to find Dean, Sal, and Roy drinking, Camille "gave us all the sad look of a harassed woman's life." Looking at Camille's painting of Galatea, Sal realizes "that all these women were spending months of loneliness and womanliness together, chatting about the madness of the men" (187). Still, there is a sense of inevitability to these gendered descriptions, as though it could not be expected that the men would be any more responsible or the women less domestic. It is worth noting as well that attention is not drawn to issues raised by the existence of the painting itself, evidence of the fact that many of these women were themselves highly creative individuals with their own genius and madness to work through. Recent collections of writing by women associated with the Beat movement and studies of their contributions to it make clear the importance of their contribution—in this prefeminist era—in ways never hinted at in this novel.

While Sal presents Camille as a pathetic figure, lying in bed crying, he presents Dean more sympathetically, "gliding around the house like Groucho Marx, with his broken thumb wrapped in a huge white bandage sticking up like a beacon that stands motionless above the frenzy of the waves" (187). His life's circumstances are presented in Sal's description of his luggage, "the beatest suitcase in the USA." His "look" is clearly that of a man living on the edge.

> He was wearing a T-shirt, torn pants hanging down his belly, tattered shoes; he had not shaved, his hair was wild and bushy, his

eyes bloodshot, and that tremendous bandaged thumb stood supported in mid-air at heart-level ... and on his face was the goofi-
est grin I ever saw. (188)

This image may seem less radical now as such styles have become fashionable and men carefully cultivate unshaven faces, with hair gelled
into planned dishevelment and expensive designer clothes in the style
of working class. In fact, old photographs of Kerouac have been used
in recent stylish clothing ads, but in the postwar era, Dean's look was
that of a man outside all the conventions of acceptability.

Beat writers were fascinated with angels and saints, and Dean
again achieves that status here. "He no longer cared about anything
(as before) but now he also *cared about everything in principle; that is
to say, it was all the same to him and he belonged to the world and
there was nothing he could do about it"* (188). This simultaneous
involvement and detachment is, for Sal, a religious resignation, and
Dean is a Beat fallen angel: "the devil himself had never fallen farther." Having fallen from respectable domesticity, Dean then turns to
Sal. The precedents for this male bonding in American culture are
numerous of course, from the earliest novels to the most recent
"buddy" movie. As they agree to travel together to Italy—another
unfulfilled agreement—they feel ennobled: no longer simple failures
and outcasts, they become "broken-down heroes of the Western
night" (190). In a bar nearby, they "decided everything—that we
would stick together and be buddies till we died." Once again, Sal
attributes a finality to the moment that is clearly illusory—no trip to
Italy ensues, nor does their commitment to each other last. But the
declaration temporarily satisfies Sal's need for permanence, certainty,
and identity, and it reasserts his sense of a decisive and radical break.

Gender issues are addressed in a number of details as they prepare to leave, beginning with their commitment to find Dean's father
and the attempt to find Remi, perhaps to free him from the waspish
Lee Ann (191). Roy Johnson, Dean's old Denver friend who agrees to
be their chauffeur for two days, is at a turning point in his life, torn
between two apparently irreconcilable poles, one domestic, responsible, and heterosexual and the other more reckless and homosocial. He

is "midway between the challenge of his new wife and the challenge of his old Denver poolhall gang leader" and, while his wife is unhappy about the arrangement, he goes along with them in order "to make a stand as the man of the house." When they arrive at the home of Galatea Dunkel, they find that her husband Ed has left her. Just as Ed and Dean "gave her the slip" months ago in a hotel lobby on a trip east, Ed has again "give[n] Galatea the slip," writes Sal, as though Ed has escaped from captivity. While Sal claims that Ed has "left out of stupors and disinclinations only" (192), Galatea herself holds Dean responsible.

Here begins a conversation that directly confronts all these tensions and conflicts, as Galatea begins to attack. "All you think about is what's hanging between your legs" (194), she says, but this only confirms Sal's own estimation that "sex was the one and only holy and important thing in [Dean's] life" (4). And Dean himself has claimed that he doesn't care about anything "so long's I can get that lil ole gal with that lil sumpin down there between her legs" (10). The charge that he is a con man who cares for nothing but his "damned kicks" (194) is of course entirely true, easy to see right from the start, and presumably forms in part the basis of his appeal. The women, accusing Dean of "just being himself," appear "sullen" and "mean" to Sal, who describes them as nothing "but a sewing circle"—apparently a term of derision—as they glare at Dean "with lowered and hating eyes" (193). As Galatea's accusations mount, he chooses not to defend himself. In spite of his legendary ability to talk his way into and out of any situation, he simply absorbs the indictment, giggling as accusations fly, and Sal resumes his mythologizing: "Dean, by virtue of his enormous series of sins, was becoming the Idiot, the Imbecile, the Saint of the lot" (193). Instead of taking life seriously and "trying to make something decent out of it," as Galatea thinks he should, Dean has become "the HOLY GOOF" (194).

Sal's defense of Dean—delivered in retrospect but not to the women in the room—leaves untouched the accusations of irresponsibility. The refusal to try to "make something decent of it" is close to Sal's recent rejection of "white ambitions," but the lines dividing men and women, particularly at this time, all too often left women in the position of paying for this male irresponsibility. Their frustrations are clear and there is no defense, but Sal is more interested, as usual, in Dean's response as he stands "in front of everybody, ragged and broken and idiotic ... saying, 'Yes, yes, yes,' as though tremendous revelations were pouring into him all the time now, and I am convinced they were, and the others suspected as much and were frightened. He was BEAT—the root, the soul of Beatific" (195). This moment combines dejection and transcendence and for Sal, the price is worth paying. "Bitterness, recriminations, advice, morality, sadness—everything was behind him, and ahead of him was the ragged and ecstatic joy of pure being." "Ragged" and "ecstatic" are the same words used only a few pages before to describe the "Negroes of America" whose community Sal longed hopelessly to join. In Dean, then, he has found his "white negro"—to borrow Norman Mailer's phrase—and a way of life beyond white ambitions and disappointments.

Afterward, Dean exudes an undiminished appetite: " 'Ah, man, don't worry, everything is perfect and fine.' He was rubbing his belly and licking his lips" (196). As if to prove the point, the next chapter sweeps men and women both into a nightlife swirl of intoxication and excitement in the African American jazz bars. The wild abandon apparently prevalent there is precisely the attitude Dean has led others to embrace, the attitude for which he has just been condemned. But even immediately following his unofficial trial and conviction, the whole group is ready to follow when Dean calls out, "Wheeoo! let's go!" and his call is answered by the "wild tenorman bawling horn ... going 'EE-YAH! EE-YAH! EE-YAH!' and hands clapping to the beat and folks yelling, 'Go, go, go' " while Dean yells, "Blow, man, blow!" Shortly before, Galatea had wished Dean dead, but now she stands on her chair with beer in hand, "shaking and jumping" along with him (196–97).

This scene provides another instance—one of the most developed—of the racial phenomenon so often referred to: admiration of African American cultural forms specifically for their suggestion of a way out of a white cultural impasse. This is definitely not the site of responsible people trying to make something decent out of life (to use Galatea's phrase), but of people who apparently exist without "yawning" and who demonstrate the capacity to transform sadness (a constant companion for Sal) into joy.

> A bunch of colored men in Saturday-night suits were whooping it up in front...a crazy place, crazy floppy women wandered around sometimes in their bathrobes, bottles clanked in alleys. In back of the joint in a dark corridor beyond the spattered toilets scores of men and women stood against the wall drinking wine-spodiodi and spitting at the stars. (196)

The tone is set by the jazz that inspired the Beat generation just as rock music would inspire the generation of the 1960s. As Thomas Pynchon has observed, the Beat movement "was a sane and decent affirmation" of American values, and when "the hippie resurgence came along ten years later.... Beat prophets were resurrected, people started playing alto sax riffs on electric guitars."[1] And, interestingly, Neal Cassady—Dean's original—was at the center of the 1960s movement as well, traveling then with Ken Kesey instead of the burnt-out Kerouac.

Dean and Sal have claimed that they no longer care about anything, and that sentiment of desperate freedom is echoed in the tenor sax "blowing at the peak of a wonderfully free idea...blasted along to the rolling crash of butt-scarred drums hammered by a big brutal Negro with a bullneck who didn't give a damn about anything" (196–97). The image of disheveled Dean earlier that day is echoed here in the image of the tenor sax player who "wore a tattered suede jacket, a purple shirt, cracked shoes, and zoot pants without press; he didn't care" (198). This abandonment of "white ambitions" promises to allow access to realms of experience unavailable to those still struggling with modernity's threats and lures, access to an intensity they felt was impossible to conceive let alone experience while committed to "making something decent" of conventional life. The path to the particular form of Beat experience so valued here runs through the feeling that nothing matters, a resignation based in sadness and despair but opening to forms of experience otherwise unavailable.

At this point, another theme connected to that realm is reintroduced: the sax player, writes Sal, "*had it* and everybody knew he had it.... They were all urging that tenorman to hold it and keep it with cries and wild eyes" (197). This "it" has come up before of course, and refers here to an ecstatic state arising from the music and the audience's rapt immersion in it, a music that—unlike the polite swing bands or the sentimentality of popular music—is visceral, powerful, expressive, simultaneously vulgar and intellectually challenging. Musicians jump and scream, stagger and fall; the audience stumbles and sweats, yells, laughs, and rocks. In this fulfillment of the roman candle vision of life, there is no chance of yawning; yet behind it is a sadness never concealed for long even in the highest flights of music and intoxication. The sax player's "big brown eyes were concerned with sadness" and "he shook his head with disgust and weariness at the whole world." His expression "seemed to say, Hey now, what's this thing we're doing in this sad brown world?" (198–99). The brownness of the earth is stressed as was the brownness of the Mississippi in the last section, and what is at stake in this "brown" man's music is "poor beat life itself in the god-awful streets of man." At the end of the song, emotionally spent, he "staggered off the platform to brood.... He looked down and wept. He was the greatest" (199).

Kerouac always preferred the "hot" style to the "cool" style that was becoming popular. The cool image, he wrote in 1959, "is your bearded laconic sage ... before a hardly touched beer in a beatnik dive, whose speech is low and unfriendly, whose girls say nothing and wear black." The hot image "is the crazy talkative shining eyed (often innocent and openhearted) nut who runs from bar to bar, pad to pad, looking for everybody, shouting, restless, lushy"("Origins," 61). At the beginning of the novel, Sal expresses his irritation with his intellectual friends and the "tired bookish or political or psychoanalytical" (10) attitudes that obstruct more spontaneous responses. When a white drummer asks to sit in, Sal is suspicious; when he plays, the suspicions are confirmed: "he began stroking the snares with soft goofy bop brushes, swaying his neck with that complacent Reichiananalyzed ecstasy that doesn't mean anything except too much tea and soft foods and goofy kicks on the cool order" (200). The dismissive reference to Reichian psychoanalysis confirms that for him possibility lay not with the continued pursuit of Euro-American intellectualism but in a "fellahin" jazz culture valuing intensity over analysis. The response of the first (hot) drummer is clear: " 'What that man doing?' he said. 'Play the music!' he said. 'What in hell!' he said. 'Shh-ee-t!' and looked away disgusted" (200).

These musicians, like the Beats whose lives they render in jazz, oscillate between two extreme conditions, and Kerouac presents before and after images of the artist possessed by intensity and the artist exhausted by intensity. The man playing "had beady, glittering eyes ... and he hopped and flopped with his horn and threw his feet around ... and he never stopped," writes Kerouac, "and it was all laughter and understanding" (201). Meanwhile, after playing, another "hornman sat absolutely motionless at a corner table with an untouched drink in front of him, staring gook-eyed into space ... his body shriveled into absolute weariness and entranced sorrow.... Everything swirled around him like a cloud" (201–2). The first, still playing, "hopped and monkeydanced with his magic horn and blew two hundred choruses of blues, each one more frantic than the other, and no signs of failing energy.... The whole room shivered" (202). This intensity, whether of exertion or of exhaustion, is all that matters and it can only be achieved through an uncompromising acceptance of the moment. The positive effect here at "the end of the continent" is "the end of doubt, all dull doubt and tomfoolery" (201) while the negative effect—a home life in ruins—was demonstrated quite clearly at the outset of the chapter.

This whole section inverts the postwar cultural trajectory about to emerge with its emphasis on racial integration and women's liberation. Sal and Dean appreciate African American culture precisely for its separation from the mainstream, and they search at times for a way to reassert traditional—almost mythical—gender roles. This is clear as they end the night of drinking with "a colored guy called Walter" (203) at his home in "the tenements." As they come in at dawn, Walter's wife is sleeping but smiles when they wake her up to continue drinking and talking. Walter's wife, writes Sal, is "the sweetest woman in the world," and as they disturb her sleep "she smiled and smiled. She never asked Walter where he'd been, what time it was, nothing." Later, when it is time to leave, they wake her again, and once again she smiles and, again, says nothing. This freedom to come and go without reproach, without spousal expectations—a specifically male freedom—is predicated on the cheerful acquiescence of the women, and this is one of the novel's clearest and most succinct examples of the essential masculinity of the Beat project. While at the end of this section Walter's nameless wife lies in her tenement bed silently smiling, never holding Walter accountable, Camille opened the section in her tenement bed with tears and accusations against Dean. Dean sums it up: "there's a *real* woman for you. Never a harsh word, never a complaint.... This is a man, and that's his castle" (203).

There is no way of glimpsing what Walter's wife might think of all this, how she and Walter feel about their tenement life, or what they might think of this envy on the part of those who had so many more opportunities available to them. The irony in characterizing a tenement with a bare lightbulb as a castle is almost lost in this moment of masculine self-congratulation. And as they wander at dawn in the "gray, ragged street" (204), a moment invoking Ginsberg's famous line in "Howl" about "angelheaded hipsters" who are "dragging themselves through the Negro streets at dawn," Sal looks around at the last straggling figures in the dawn's early light, and his vision is transformative: "Holy flowers floating in the air, were all these tired faces in the dawn of Jazz America" (204). This Jazz America was an alternative America, a subterranean America invisible from the mainstream but coming into view as "white ambitions" are jettisoned and the intoxications, the highs and lows of "fellahin" freedom are accepted.

The last main character to speak in the chapter is Galatea, whose earlier criticism lends a context to Dean's admiration for Walter and his silent, smiling wife. After the excitement of the night before she still wishes Dean would "go on one of these trips and never come back," but she has modified her approach and lost some of her certainty: "When Ed gets back I'm going to take him to Jameson's Nook [jazz bar] every night and let him get his fill of madness. Do you think that'll work, Sal? I don't know what to do" (205). It is perhaps worth noting that the real-life counterparts for Galatea and Ed Dunkel, Al and Helen Hinkle, remained together for many years until Helen's death in 1995. Novelist Joyce Johnson, Kerouac's lover at the time of the publication of *On the Road*, argues in her very insightful memoir

Minor Characters that these attitudes toward gender are best judged in their historical context. At the beginning of a period of enormous reevaluation, women such as Helen Hinkle, Carolyn Cassady, and others were part of an important transition, "a bridge to the next generation, who in the 1960s, when a young woman's right to leave home was no longer an issue, would question every assumption that limited women's lives and begin the long, never-to-be-completed work of transforming relationships with men."[2]

In an almost cinematic conclusion to this crucial section of the narrative, as Sal heads off to meet Dean in order to continue their journey, the narrative lens draws back to provide a larger picture—as occurred in the description of the mountains around Denver. This picture represents one of the most positive elements of Kerouac's America—the city: Mission Street "was a great riot of construction work, children playing, whooping Negroes coming home from work, dust, excitement, the great buzzing and vibrating hum of what is really America's most excited city—and overhead the pure blue sky and the joy of the foggy sea that always rolls in at night to make everybody hungry for food and further excitement" (205). Kerouac's inner city is often a space of energy and eclecticism, spontaneity and creativity, and works such as *On the Road* contributed to a new interest in urban life that drew many people back into the downtown areas in later decades, slowing the trend to the suburbs.

The next day, as they leave San Francisco, Sal and Dean return to the subject of "it." When a musician has "it," according to Dean, he can express "what's on everybody's mind. . . . he rises to his fate and has to blow equal to it." When this aesthetic magic happens, "everybody looks up and knows; they listen; he picks it up and carries. Time stops. He's filling empty space with the substance of our lives" (206). The music is a means to an end: a heightened state of consciousness in which "we know what IT is and we know TIME and we know that everything is really FINE," declares Dean. In this condition, time, always a concern in this novel, becomes unthreatening, at least for this moment. For the others in the car though, time is an endless source of worry and anxiety: how many miles to go, where to sleep, how much money, the weather, and so on. With their anxieties and preoccupations, these people "betray time"—the opposite of the musician who has "it"—"and all the time it all flies by them and they know it and that *too* worries them no end" (208–9). As Sal has already realized, it is not possible both to remain open to a transcendent "it" and to pursue the mundane "white" ambitions of a Middle American patriarch.

In telling their childhood stories, Sal and Dean try to capture the energy, intensity, and abandon of the improvisational jazz they admire. This attempt confronts the problem of time both by transcending it at the moment of performance, according to Dean, and by recovering it in the memories they bring to the surface of consciousness. Swept up in a frenzied recounting of their lives, they push to the limit their ability to articulate meaning and project identity: "Dean and I both swayed to the rhythm and the IT of our final excited joy in talking and living to the blank tranced end of all innumerable riotous angelic particulars that had been lurking in our souls all our lives" (208). The sense of endings multiplies here: at "the end of the continent," at the end of the night, in a "final joy," they have found "the end of doubt, all dull doubt," and now at the "blank tranced end" they approach another ecstatic moment. This discussion of "IT" leads into a demonstration as Dean's ability to improvise and respond instantly is displayed in his driving skills, a genre of improvisational performance art in itself that terrifies the other passengers (210). And it is a musical comparison Sal makes to describe the driving: going through the mountains, he is "passing everybody and never halting the rhythmic advance that the mountains themselves intended" (211). In his spontaneity, Dean is once again in tune with nature itself—with "IT"—rather than being slowed down and having his life's rhythm upset by time-betraying anxieties.

Time is a major factor here, producing the sense of loss and sadness that permeates the book in the characters' inability to hold on to the past, their search for absent fathers, the separation anxiety experienced as friends recede from view, the loss of childhood innocence, and the moments of perfect intensity when time disappears. Sal's way of dealing with time is suggested in his myth of the rainy night: on one level, there is no escape from the sense of immediate loss; but on another level, time is a fluid and cyclical process of death and rebirth that allows the possibility of a transcendent and harmonious vision. This vision is one that Sal elaborates at various levels—personal, cultural, and cosmic. While Sal is fascinated by Dean's strategy for dealing with time, his own strategy is very different. Dean hopes to escape from the anxieties of temporality by living as intensely as possible in the present moment, immersing himself so fully in immediate sensations and desires that all extraneous doubts, commitments, worries, and obligations are obscured from view. Dean's rhapsodic philosophical visions cannot be separated from his application of this philosophy, however, and on this trip east, some problematic consequences of this attitude are considered. He cares little for conventional morality and is willing to do anything to keep his momentum; if this means taking advantage of people, he has no hesitation in doing so.

Near Denver, scene of his youth, Dean reverts to a wildness that nothing in the novel so far has entirely revealed. The previous instances of petty theft at roadside gas stations and stores seem tame compared to this reversion to his wild juvenile delinquent tendencies. He tries to trade sex for money. He lusts after the 13-year-old girl whose mother, Frankie, has kindly put them up, for example, "watching her with slitted eyes" (218) until Sal warns him away from her and protects her from him. His desire for a neighbor's daughter results in death threats from a shotgun-toting mother. As they drink hard, Dean begins crazily stealing cars for joyrides as he had done in his youth, barely eluding the police he so fears. "All the bitterness and madness of his entire Denver life was blasting out of his system like daggers. His face was red and sweaty and mean" (221). By the end, as in New York prior to another departure, "Everything was in a horrible mess, all of Denver, my woman friend, cars, children, poor Frankie, the living room spattered with beer and cans" (222), and it is time to leave before police and neighbors catch up with Dean. Certainly, in light of these results, Dean's approach to time must be viewed with at least some caution.

Sal's approach is quite different, and the difference is evident in his response to this same situation. The term "Okie" (Oklahoman) refers to the many people displaced by the depression and the dust bowl, and the "Okie family" they stay with impresses him greatly. The most famous portrait of such people is Steinbeck's *The Grapes of Wrath,* and like Steinbeck, Kerouac sees an undiminished appetite for life in these people on the margins of society. In a letter written around this time, Kerouac complained that "the East is really effete.... Say anything you want, I like my people joy-hearted. It is the sickly-heartedness of the East that has finally driven me away" (*Letters,* 190). As in his description of Terry and her Chicana life, Walter and his tenement life, Sal now looks to Colorado "Okies" for an antidote. Abandoned by her husband, Frankie "was a wonderful woman in jeans who drove coal trucks in winter mountains to support her kids" (214). Her life is much to Sal's liking, as it has included "many a good time and a big Sunday-afternoon drunk in crossroads bars and laughter and guitar-playing in the night." Growing up in these surroundings, Frankie's children, according to Sal, are "wonderful," curious about nature, poetic, creative. Unaffected by social pretension or the desire to conform, this family "lived their ragged and joyous lives" despite the disapproval of their more appearance-conscious neighbors. Once again, the word *ragged* indicates not only material deprivation but also the possibility of freedom, openness, and vision. Life here may be lived outside the more tightly woven confines of propriety, but it makes available a broader and richer perspective:

> At night all the lights of Denver lay like a great wheel on the plain below, for the house was in that part of the West where the mountains roll down foothilling to the plain and where in primeval times soft waves must have washed from sea-like Mississippi to make such round and perfect stools for the island-peaks like Evans and Pike and Longs.

This reference to the Mississippi returns to the myth of the rainy night, to the cyclic and transitory condition of nature, and to a vast sense of time that dwarfs both Dean's manic and petty lusts and the neighbors' concerns with a tidy yard.

Kerouac's desire for this kind of life remained mostly unrealized. Not long before the real events that are fictionalized in this section of *On the Road,* Kerouac wrote to Ginsberg from Denver that he had decided "to become a Thoreau of the Mountains. To live like Jesus and Thoreau, except for women. Like Nature Boy with his Nature Girl." This notion is based on romantic and unrealizable versions of the West, but it gives a glimpse of Kerouac's state of mind, of the lines of thought he was following in trying to invent yet another new identity. "I'll wander the wild, wild mountains and wait for Judgment Day," he writes. "I believe there will be a Judgment Day, but not for men ... *for society*. Society is a mistake.... I don't believe at all in this society. It is evil. It will fall. Men have to do what they want" (*Letters,* 193). In the same letter, Kerouac refers to Burroughs's equally apocalyptic opinion that "the human race will become extinct if it doesn't stop doing what it doesn't want to do" (*Letters,* 191).

This failure of people to do what they want is noted several times in this part of *On the Road*. After his attempt to hustle a gay driver, Dean complains, "Offer them what they secretly want and they of course immediately become panic-stricken" (209). Soon after, he adds "the moment it comes to act, this paralysis, scared, hysterical, nothing frightens em more than what they *want*" (215). Some people know what they want, but for some reason cannot do it; others have a deeper problem. Sal converses later in the trip for example "with a gorgeous country girl" who only seems to know "what one should do" (242), not what she wants to do. "Her great dark eyes surveyed me with emptiness and a kind of chagrin that reached back generations and generations in her blood from not having done what was crying to be done." Try as he might, Sal cannot find out what she wants other than the ordinary life of working America. "She didn't know. She yawned. She was sleepy.... She was eighteen and most lovely, and lost" (243). Sal has declared his interest in those "who never yawn or say a commonplace thing" (8) from the start, and this young woman—like Rita Bettencourt, who also yawned—baffles and saddens him.

The possibility that many people actually do want to live "ordinary" lives seems not to occur to Sal, fixed as he is on his romantic ideas of living on the edge, of marginality, alienation, and transcendence. Dean appears to be the embodiment of a man who does what he wants to do whatever the cost, who is guided by the pleasure principle, and who has rejected "the logical, sober but hateful sanity" (*Letters,* 191) that obstructs desire. What did Kerouac want? It changed frequently of course, but in the 1949 letter to Ginsberg, he rejects not only middle America but also urban hipster life in favor of a more peaceful and pastoral option. The repetitive rhetoric of the passage makes clear the crucial importance of articulating desire itself.

> I want to be left alone. I want to sit in the grass. I want to ride my horse. I want to lay a woman naked in the grass on the mountainside. I want to think. I want to pray. I want to sleep. I want to look at the stars. I want what I want. I want to prepare my own food, with my own hands, and live that way. I want to roll my own. I want to smoke some deermeat and pack it in my saddlebag, and go away over the bluff. I want to read books. I want to write books. (*Letters,* 194)

But desire, in modern America, appears blocked like the Mississippi in the novel's last section. "It's all wrong," Kerouac declares, "and I denounce it and it can go to hell. I don't believe in this society." He goes on to reject education and culture, concluding that "History is people doing what their leaders tell them; and not doing what their prophets tell them. Life is what gives you desires but no rights for the fulfillment of desires." These ideas would find their most responsive audience in the late 1960s when thousands of young people, reading books like *On the Road* and *The Dharma Bums,* decided that American modernity was foundering and sought, however naively, new and radical ways to live in harmony with desire and nature.

If Kerouac is thinking of Thoreau, he casts Dean in a Melville role: a "mad Ahab at the wheel" driving at "incredible speeds across the groaning continent" (234). This reference to Ahab, the monomaniacal captain in Melville's *Moby Dick,* willing to risk annihilation for his desire to pursue the white whale, juxtaposes Dean and Sal with Ahab and Ishmael. Like *Moby Dick, On the Road* is a first-person narrative of an extreme voyage outside mainstream America and one that considers the apocalyptic end of "white" civilization. And Kerouac was quite aware of the importance of this allusion: "I'm making *On the Road* a kind of Melvillean thing, in spite of myself," he wrote in a 1949 letter (*Letters,* 205). The next chapter begins with a passage echoing briefly the opening of *Moby Dick* and Ishmael's restless discontent: "Whenever spring comes to New York I can't stand the suggestions of the land that come blowing over the river from New Jersey and I've got to go" (249). This journey, like Melville's, is as much metaphoric as geographic: "Sal, we gotta go and never stop going till we get there" says Dean. "Where we going, man?" replies Sal. "I don't know but we gotta go," he answers (238), and on they go into the Chicago night that Sal had glimpsed on his first trip west, a bop Chicago of jazz, kicks, and "It." Here, Sal reverses the sense of ending he faced not long before as he realizes again that there is no end, no final word: "There's always more, a little further—it never ends" (241).

In Detroit, Sal's wrestling with identity reaches an extreme limit, an exemplary moment of Beat consciousness and experience. Without money for a room or warm clothes for a night in the park, he and Dean opt for a skid-row movie theater where they can sleep and watch B movies all night. "The people who were in that all-night movie were the end," Sal observes (243), again employing a term of finality, and the moment marks an end point of all the Hollywood references accumulating in the novel:

> Beat Negroes who'd come up from Alabama to work in car factories on a rumor; old white bums; young longhaired hipsters who'd reached the end of the road and were drinking wine; whores, ordinary couples, housewives with nothing to do, nowhere to go, nobody to believe in. If you sifted all Detroit in a wire basket the beater solid core of dregs couldn't be better gathered. (243–44)

Here again we see a definition of Beat that removes it far from the hip intellectual mavericks of New York. What follows is perhaps the most surreal moment in the novel, as the Hollywood movies play over and over all night and Sal slips in and out of sleep, a "horrible osmotic experience." The Hollywood images on the surface play off against the deeper disquiet of the audience, where "People slugged out of bottles and turned around and looked everywhere in the dark theater for something to do, someone to talk to.... everyone was guiltily quiet" (244). The disjunction between Hollywood's manufactured reality and the reality experienced on the outside was illustrated earlier, when Sal made sandwiches in a Hollywood parking lot, and now the gulf is even wider. Already disoriented from the frantic traveling, Sal slips in and out of sleep and in and out of the movies until his sense of identity is eroded:

> In the gray dawn that puffed ghostlike about the windows of the theater and hugged its eaves I was sleeping with my head on the wooden arm of a seat as six attendants of the theater converged with their night's total of swept-up rubbish and created a huge dusty pile that reached my nose as I snored head down—till they almost swept me away too.... All the cigarette butts, the bottles, the matchbooks, the come and the gone were swept up in this pile. Had they taken me with it, Dean would never have seen me again. He would have had to roam the entire United States and look in every garbage pail from coast to coast before he found me embryonically convoluted among the rubbishes of my life, his life, and the life of everybody concerned and not concerned. What would I have said to him from my rubbish womb? 'Don't bother me, man. I'm happy where I am. You lost me one night in Detroit in August nineteen forty-nine. What right have you to come and disturb my reverie in this pukish can?' (244–45)

Sal's sense of self as garbage to be disposed of—engulfed in filth as Kerouac was when trying on clothes that smelled of "Skid Row, puke, sperm, and sadness" (*Letters,* 121)—is curiously offset by the images of birth, womb, and embryo that are woven into the passage. Thus, it is still possible to discern the cyclical movement of his myth of the rainy night with its acceptance of the inevitability of death as a precondition of birth. The Beat fascination with, identification with, "the dregs" is radically extended here, however. To dramatize this abjection, Sal tells of a night in Boston when he "was the star in one of the filthiest dramas of all time" (245). Having got thoroughly drunk in a sailors' bar, he went "to the toilet, where I wrapped myself around the toilet bowl and went to sleep. During the night at least a hundred seamen and assorted civilians came in and cast their sentient debouchments on me till I was unrecognizably caked. What difference does it make after all?" (245). It is difficult to imagine a more abject position,

a more absolute annihilation of self than this. Sal has previously identified with those who are socially rejected and excluded, but this goes
much further; the toilet is the receptacle of all that is rejected and
excluded by the body, and Sal's acceptance of this space of disgust signals an utter abandonment of self. His drunken unconsciousness is
itself a negation of conscious selfhood; and the fact that those who
find him there leave him caked in their spit and urine indicates the
profoundest alienation. He has been misrecognized on several occa-
sions, but now his unrecognizability, even to himself, equals a total
loss of identity, the extinguishing of self, and while there is a hint of
rebirth in this passage, it is unclear what sort of rebirth it would be.

As Sal and Dean continue their journey east, Sal does not seem
to approach any form of salvation or transcendence: he feels like "a
traveling salesman—raggedy travelings, bad stock, rotten beans in the
bottom of my bag of tricks, nobody buying" (245). While some religious traditions predicate liberation on a denial of self, Sal seems not
to have achieved that. Instead the self resumes its operations as the
journey simply continues and they arrive in New York, where he
returns to his aunt's house for shelter, and Dean, "all troubles and
ecstasy and speed," (247) finds yet another woman. In this novel
obsessed with finality, there is no real finality to be had.

8

The Final Journey

Part 4 records the novel's final trip, one that takes Sal to a new level in his search for a space outside modernity. This time he goes to Mexico to locate the "fellahin" people whose culture testifies to the historical continuity of this ulterior space. As he says good-bye, Dean predicts they will both end up as "old bums"—the closest approximation to the ahistorical "fellahin" condition that white modernity affords and a prefiguring of the 1960s notion of "dropping out." "There's no harm ending that way. You spend a whole life of non-interference with the wishes of others, including politicians and the rich, and nobody bothers you and you cut along and make your own way.... It's an anywhere road for anybody anyhow" (251). The ideal of noninterference may have its merits but sounds strange coming from a man capable of interfering greatly in the lives of those around him—particularly the women he married and abandoned. This does not really play a part in his calculation of interference, however. In any case, there seems to be no way off this road for them, given "the raggedy madness and riot of our actual lives, our actual night, the hell of it, the senseless nightmare road. All of it inside endless and beginningless emptiness" (254). They part with one of Sal's customary poignant descriptions of departure:

"Suddenly he bent to his life and walked quickly out of sight. I gaped into the bleakness of my own days" (254).

This bleakness dissipates when Sal arrives in Denver though, as a round of parties with his old friends and visits to "crazy Negro saloons" (258) occupy his attention until he hears that Dean has decided to join him, abandoning another wife for Sal and the road. Sal's mythicizing tendency, always powerful, is never more present than in this description of Dean, not as a "Holy Goof" now, but as a much more powerful figure. Sal imagines him as

> a burning shuddering frightful Angel, palpitating toward me across the road, approaching like a cloud, with enormous speed, pursuing me like the Shrouded Traveler on the plain, bearing down on me. I saw his huge bony face over the plains with the mad bony purpose and the gleaming eyes; I saw his wings; I saw his old jalopy chariot with thousands of sparking flames shooting out from it; I saw the path it burned over the road ... [and] over the corn, through cities, destroying bridges, drying rivers.... Behind him charred ruins smoked. (259)

This description portrays Dean as a death figure, an avenging angel, and certainly he has played a central role in Sal's collapsing self. Here, he is connected to a sense of the impending decline of the West (to borrow Spengler's title) that will be explored further in this section. By now, Dean's reputation has grown to the point where his approaching presence instills a sense of awe in those who await him. He has become larger than life: "It was like the imminent arrival of Gargantua," Sal observes with a reference to Rabelais and his hyperbolic imagery, "preparations had to be made to widen the gutters of Denver and foreshorten certain laws to fit his suffering bulk and bursting ecstasies" (259).

The real object of the trip to Mexico is made clear in Dean's excited declaration, "Man, this will finally take us to IT!" (266). "It" has repeatedly been associated with "the end" in one form or another: the end of the continent, the end of the night, the end of consciousness, the end of time. In one sense, this statement can be read as just another in the series of announcements of finality that somehow always dissolve. Yet this time, if only because the book is itself drawing to an end, the claim seems more authoritative. The actual departure scene combines this apocalyptic mood with Sal's customary separation anxiety, the same sense of almost metaphysical loss that Sal has invoked before. He looks "back to watch Tim Gray recede on the plain.... He grew smaller and smaller, and still he stood motionless ... and I was twisted around to see more of Tim Gray till there was nothing but a growing absence in space" (267). This anxiety is reinforced in the reference to another in the series of white-haired prophetic figures, versions of the Shrouded Traveler identified previously as an emissary of death (124): "But he was coming closer to me, if only ever just behind" (268). And this time, following a reference to the lost civilization of Atlantis, the sense of ending is extended to include the city itself and the culture of which it is a part: "Denver receded back of us like the city of salt, her smokes breaking up in the air and dissolving to our sight" (268). There are several relevant biblical sources for this image of God's vengeance on those who have turned away, including this apocalyptic Old Testament vision: "the whole land thereof is brimstone, and salt, and burning...like the overthrow of Sodom, and Gomorrah" (Deut. 29:23). As Sal leaves, of course, like Lot's wife, he always looks back.

As ever, this absence is replaced by the onrush of the present as Sal and his companions hurtle south toward Mexico. Dean, Sal, and Stan Shephard arrive in Laredo, ready to cross the border, and Sal invokes the sense of social dregs that haunted him in Detroit. "It was the bottom and the dregs of America where all the heavy villains sink, where disoriented people have to go to be near a specific elsewhere they can slip into unnoticed" (274). Sal has long sought an "elsewhere" and has already imagined himself dissolved into these dregs, and now, instead of being swept up into a "pukish can" negating his identity (245), there is another option. The possibility of a new beginning hinted at then in the idea of the "rubbish womb" seems to open at the border as the end of one country is the beginning of another: "Just across the street Mexico began. We looked with wonder" (274). The police have been symbols of repression throughout the novel, enforcing the imperative to do what one should rather than what one wants, but as they enter Mexico Dean senses a different police mentality: " 'See how the *cops* are in this country. I can't believe it!' He rubbed his eyes. 'I'm dreaming' " (275). Later, when the police come to question them, the difference is clear; unlike the police encountered north of the border, the police are not there to repress but to protect. "Such lovely policemen God hath never wrought in America. No suspicions, no fuss, no bother: he was the guardian of the sleeping town, period" (295).

It seems to be a dream come true: cheap beer and cigarettes, relaxed laws, no police intimidation. Sal's expectations run extremely high at this point, and it seems that Dean's anticipation is justified: "Behind us lay the whole of America and everything Dean and I had previously known about life, and life on the road. We had finally found the magic land at the end of the road and we never dreamed the extent of the magic" (276). For now, Mexico represents the way out of the American dilemma of "white ambitions" that Sal has been seeking, and they feel utterly elated at the sense of possibility that opens up for them once they leave the United States: " 'It's the world,' said Dean. 'My God!' he cried slapping the wheel. 'It's the world!... Think of it! Son-of-a-*bitch*! Gawd-*damn*!' " (277). A more realistic note is added by the presence of Stan, "who'd been to foreign countries before, [and] just calmly slept in the back seat" (276), in contrast to Sal and Dean, who feel they have not simply crossed a political border but broken through to another way of life. Lacking any political sense of poverty as remediable oppression, Dean sees small dwellings along the road and observes, "Real beat huts, man.... These people don't *bother* with appearances" (277). Having grown up in poverty himself and having no desire for material security nor any sense that he should provide it for his family, he sees Mexican poverty simply as a release from the pressure to, as Galatea put it, "make something decent" (197). He displays no insight into Mexican culture, politics, or history, and understands it only in terms of his own situation. While he does appreciatively consider the families he sees in their homes, for example the old men who are "so cool" (278), his strongest enthusiasms are for the fact that people do not seem suspicious of him and, of course, for "Gurls, gurls."

Sal's first responses are different. As he watches a peasant with a burro, his romantic nature—seen clearly during the episode with Terry or the "old Negro plodding" with his mule—returns powerfully: "The sun rose pure on pure and ancient activities of human life" (278). This journey has, for Sal, been a journey in time as well as space, one that takes him not just south of the border but also back to the "ancient activities" of an earlier civilization whose purity has not been sacrificed to what he sees as the repressive exigencies of modernity. Sal and Dean understand Mexico as "primitive," comments Hunt, and for them, this is meant to be a positive term: "Its people live in a manner so old and fundamental that they are before history and timeless" (Hunt 1996, 62). It seems as though the promise suggested in the rubbish womb metaphor has been fulfilled in a sense—Sal has at last fallen through the dregs at the bottom into a space of purity. Having left Denver, a city apparently under threat of destruction from God's wrath, he has come with Dean, an avenging angel, to a land that in his view has not abandoned the ancient and pure path, not yet experienced the fall into modernity. The novel's ongoing concern with temporality is addressed here as well, as the archaic "fellahin" life is contrasted with the historical: "As essential as rocks in the desert are they in the desert of 'history,' " Sal comments (281). Mexican culture, which seems to Sal to have remained more or less unchanged for centuries, thus provides a solidity to temporal experience that otherwise recedes—like history itself—into the past and is lost, like all the people Sal leaves behind.

This is not like any trip they have taken in the United States. While previous journeys have had their moments of intensity and vision, those moments appeared as oases in the desert of American modernity. Here, however, they feel that they have arrived at the source, "where we would finally learn ourselves among the Fellahin Indians of the world, the essential strain of the basic primitive, wailing humanity that stretches in a belt around the equatorial belly of the world." Malaya, India, Arabia, Morocco, Mexico, Polynesia, and Siam are mentioned as parts of this worldwide "fellahin" culture, all closely related to each other and free from the taint of "civilization." As this passage makes clear, Sal does not really feel himself in Mexico per se, so much as he feels he has entered a global "fellahin" space. In his mind—the mind of a reluctant citizen of Spengler's imperial culture—the differences separating these various cultures are insignificant in comparison to their shared difference from modernity: "you hear the same mournful wail by the rotted walls of Cádiz, Spain, that you hear 12,000 miles around in the depths of Benares" (280). African American jazz now appears as another permutation of the single archaic source of all this music in Sal's unifying concept of the "fellahin." "The mambo beat [in Mexico] is the conga beat from Congo, the river of Africa and the world; it's really the world beat" (287). This is probably the first usage of the phrase "world beat," a designation that has more recently come into vogue signifying various musical forms originating outside the modern Euro-American tradition.

Sal's respect for these people allows him to penetrate the racist American clichés and stereotypes that so often reduce and mock them, an important accomplishment at this moment in cultural history. "These people were unmistakably Indians," he asserts, "and were not at all like the Pedros and Panchos of silly civilized American lore ... they were not fools, they were not clowns" (281). Yet that same respect allows him to impose on them a heavy symbolic function of his own, one that threatens equally to obscure actual people from view: "they were great grave Indians and they were the source of mankind and the fathers of it." The whole novel has been haunted by absent fathers, and in these Indians Sal claims at last to have found a collective paternity. Dean is always searching for his father while running away from his own role as a father to his own children. Sal's own attempt to style himself as a patriarch in Denver ends in the annihilation of self in a skid-row Detroit movie theater. Here the image moves from the level of the individual to the level of culture as Sal now finds the fathers whose absence has been keenly felt as recently as the day of their departure from Denver. Sal sees himself reflected in the critical gaze of these patriarchs: "And they knew this when we passed, ostensibly self-important moneybag Americans on a lark in their land; they knew who was the father and who was the son of antique life on earth, and made no comment" (281).

Here Sal's Spenglerian sense of history with its vision of the rise and decline of the Euro-American empires, finds its culmination in the timeless continuity of "fellahin" culture, although he approves it in a way that Spengler, no admirer of the ahistorical "fellahin," would never have countenanced. Sal's first journey began with his research into American history, and his concern with time has remained strong, but now he seems to have arrived at a transcendence of history itself. If Sal sees history as a road leading from the primitive to the modern, then he feels that he is approaching the beginning point of that road, a stable point of origin. Thus history, the sense of linear time vanishing into the past like Sal's repeated departure images, is resolved in the figure of the timeless "fellahin" for whom history does not exist in any meaningful way. "These were my growing thoughts as I drove in the hot sunbaked town of Gregoria," Sal records (281), and they are crucial thoughts both to the development of this novel and to the cultural upheaval in the 1960s (that *On the Road* helped set in motion) concerning countercultural attitudes toward "primitive" cultures. Kerouac's idealization of the "fellahin"—indeed the very coherence of the concept itself—must be called into question in this postcolonial age, but there is no doubt about the importance of such notions at that time.

It is startling to follow Sal and Dean, in the very next paragraph, as they visit a Mexican brothel where all Sal's sensitive thinking dissolves in a day of debauchery. Here it is at last possible to do what one wants, it seems, rather than what one should, and the police remain uninvolved. The necessity of restrained behavior that accompanies white middle-class respectability is transformed into its opposite, a carnivalesque indulgence in transgressive sexuality, alcohol, and drug consumption—behavior that Sal associates with the freedom of lowered expectations supposedly experienced by the "fellahin." That this space is constructed as freedom from a white male point of view, however, does not mean that it can be understood that way for anyone else, a point that emerges as Sal notes the sadness and despair of the young prostitute whose "awful grief" drives her to outrageous alcoholic consumption, who fixes "poor sunken lost eyes" on him as she begs for money and drinks (288–89). Yet his (un)critical analysis of the situation stops there, leaving her grief as an aesthetic or existential effect rather than placing it in political or cultural context. The descriptions of the scene, the frequently noted skin colors of the "girls," place this narrative episode within the now-familiar racial and gender category of orientalist discourse whose contours of power Edward Said has traced. Sal compares the experience to an "Arabian dream," for example, "Ali Baba and the alleys and the courtesans" (289). Orientalist imagery pervades the entire scene: they approach the bar "through narrow Algerian streets" (286), and when it is time to go, they "still wanted to hang around with our lovely girls in this strange Arabian paradise" until Sal finally recalls that he is "in Mexico after all and not in a pornographic hasheesh daydream" (290–91).[1]

As they leave, Sal reflects blithely that they had "left joys and celebrations over hundreds of pesos behind us, and it didn't seem like a bad day's work" (291). Perhaps some perspective on all this may be gained in light of Sal's earlier comment about "self-important money-bag Americans on a lark" (281), but in any case the hedonism displayed here demonstrates little empathy with the "fellahin" people he has met and can be ascribed perhaps to the excesses of American modernity that Sal critiques even as he enjoys them. Despite his admiration for the Mexicans he meets, there is a vast cultural gap here, and it is compounded by the fact that Sal and Dean so rarely seem to be aware of it. "It was hard to come around without a common language," Sal does admit at one point though and so the Americans and Mexicans "mused separate national and racial and personal high-eternity thoughts" (284). It is true that at this time awareness of Mexican culture that would contribute to a sounder understanding was not readily available, but Sal's earlier renunciation of cultural clichés suggests that he will overcome them, not replace them with a new set. The imperative often expressed in the novel to do what one wants rather than what one should do often leads to morally questionable or reprehensible behavior, and here this is certainly the case. It could be argued, for example, that the problem arises not simply because they should repress their desires but because their desires should be informed by more knowledge, more empathy, and so on.

The farther they travel, the more they leave "civilized" American culture behind in a journey whose trajectory somewhat resembles Conrad's *Heart of Darkness* with the difference that Kerouac's first-person narrator—unlike Conrad's Marlowe—sees the "uncivilized" as the repository of wisdom, sanity, and stability. The road itself is a modern construct and a manifestation of the very civilization they are escaping though, so the limits of their escape are maintained by their presence on the road. "They probably, off the road, over that bluff, miles back, must be even wilder and stranger, yeah, because the Pan-American Highway partially civilizes this nation on this road," says Dean (297). His curiosity is strong: "How different they must be in their private concerns and evaluations and wishes," he says (298), but there is little sense that he will ever really get "off the road" long enough to address these questions seriously any more than he learned anything about the African American with the mule wagon (113). The fact that their friend Chad King has become an anthropologist (269) suggests another approach to these questions, but this is an academic road they will not travel. In any case, the knowledge Sal seeks is neither academic nor objective, nor is it really even primarily related to Mexico or Indians so much as to Sal's own psyche. The Indian girls seem familiar: "Their great brown, innocent eyes looked into ours with such soulful intensity.... They were like the eyes of the Virgin Mother when she was a child. We saw in them the tender and forgiving gaze of Jesus. And they stared unflinchingly into ours" (298). Sal translates their presence into religious terms of his own, and in these "fellahin" figures he finds an image of salvation—the fulfillment of his name, Sal Paradise. The land itself seems to reflect this condition as well, and in another account of this trip south—in *Visions of Cody*—Kerouac refers to Mexico as "God's original Eden jungle" and to the "Fellaheen Eternal Country Life" that exists there.[2]

One of Kerouac's stated intentions in writing *On the Road* was to examine the relation of his generation to history. On one level, he writes in a plot synopsis of the novel, it is "a story of many restless travelings and at the same time an imaginative survey of a new American generation known as the 'Hip' (The Knowing), with emphasis on their problems in the mid-century." Kerouac wanted also to examine "their historical relationship with preceding generations.... This new generation has a conviction that it alone has known everything, or been 'hip,' in the history of the world" (*Letters,* 226). One characteristic distinguishing Kerouac from the "hip" and urban literary scene he knew so well was his belief that the smug superiority of some of these urban sophisticates and modern intellectuals was absolutely misguided. Throughout the novel, the most valuable forms of knowledge are invariably located outside the standard and official channels of the white American culture that was coming to dominate the world, spreading "history" itself farther and farther outward from the roads. And, Kerouac believed, this empire would not last. As he declares in *Visions of Cody,* "The future's in Fellaheen" (380).

There is, toward the end of the novel, an apocalyptic vision of a future which can be taken to frame, in a sense, the whole narrative and its understanding of cultural history. Sal and Dean experience a powerful sense of cultural difference as they pass through "Strange crossroad towns" and encounter "shawled Indians watching us under hatbrims" (299). "Life was dense, dark, ancient," observes Sal, pointing out again the timeless quality that, in his view, distinguishes "fellahin" life. But modernity is spreading, tainting traditional cultures with new forms of desire, and as these "self-important moneybag Americans on a lark" pass by, modern forms of desire are kindled. The Indians reach out their hands, begging for "something they thought civilization could offer," but, Sal reflects, "they never dreamed the sadness and poor broken disillusion of it. They didn't know that a bomb had come that could crack all our bridges and roads and reduce them to jumbles, and we would be as poor as they someday" (299). It is not just coincidental that this vision of destruction contains some of the same terms employed to describe the arrival of Dean as avenging angel in Denver, or that the final image of Denver suggests a city destroyed. Just as Dean himself appears more and more as an apocalyptic figure linking urban America with the "fellahin"—a sign of Spenglerian decline—here, with a vision of nuclear holocaust, the gap between civilized and "fellahin" is finally closed.

This is Kerouac's version of the conclusion to modernity as predicted by Spengler—the literal and sudden decline of western civilization—but again with a twist. In Kerouac's rendition, the decline is also a return to an ancient and unified source:

> For when destruction comes to the world of "history" and the
> Apocalypse of the Fellahin returns once more as so many times
> before, people will still stare with the same eyes from the caves of
> Mexico as well as from the caves of Bali, where it all began and
> where Adam was suckled and taught to know. (281)

This is the fulfillment of Sal's desire to put an end to his bourgeois life, his "white ambitions." Just as they began there, all history's roads lead back to the "fellahin," and in *On the Road,* modern western history leads inevitably to its own destruction—"bridges and roads" reduced to jumbles—and thence to ultimate reunion with the "fellahin," with the brown people and the brown earth with whom Sal has identified for so long. And in this vision, the myth of the rainy night with its brown river finds its historical or cultural analogue, as transitory history delivers modernity back to its timeless source and the cycle continues.

Given the sense of finality and understanding, of both closure and new beginning, that marks this section, it is surprising that the powerful impact one might expect does not occur. The arrival in Mexico City is almost like a homecoming in that it appears to be the city made for them, a Beat city. "This was the great and final wild uninhibited Fellahin-childlike city that we knew we would find at the end of the road" (302), Sal concludes at the end of a long and breathless passage describing the atmosphere there. But within a paragraph, Sal is sick with dysentery, Dean is saying good-bye and heading back to New York, and the rest of Sal's stay in Mexico receives no narration at all. This is an abrupt end to what might have been the novel's great moment of epiphany, providing the resolution of all that has come before. While all the narrative of the trip to Mexico City seems to prepare for some closure, in the end no resolution is offered, and the experience appears as another example of the "magical action for naught" (173). Sal seems to have absorbed nothing lasting from his "fellahin" experience, at least nothing that has any visible impact on his life and attitudes.

It has been argued that the Mexican section is essentially repetition, this time against an exotic backdrop, but this misses an important, even crucial point. By setting the final episode in Mexico among the "fellahin," and making reference to the bomb—a major preoccu-pation of the time—Kerouac's revision of the Spenglerian historical pattern is made clear. Sal is part of a civilization in decline, possibly on the verge of blowing itself up, if not of sinking into an irreversible cul-tural decline. Historical cycles of rise and fall have occurred in the past and will occur in the future, and it would be a mistake to think that white Euro-American civilization would somehow be exempt from this process. While Sal (and Kerouac) may not find a way to a personal rebirth, the presence of the timeless "fellahin" guarantees that the process will continue. In the vast cycles of history, the decline of the West will have no appreciable effect on "the great fellahin peo-ples of the world," who manifest whatever hope remains in a world destroying itself by its blind adherence to modern "white ambitions."

In part 5, Sal is abruptly back in New York, involved with yet another woman who is introduced as his true love: "there she was, the girl with the pure and innocent dear eyes that I had searched for and for so long. We agreed to love each other madly" (306). By this time, his sudden declaration of final love is not much more believable than the statement that "Dean's life was settled" (308) as he returns to Camille and his children in San Francisco. The state of confusion that reigns around Sal and Dean during their last meeting here suggests that "the raggedy madness and riot of our actual lives" (254) will con-tinue indefinitely. Sal may have glimpsed the future in Mexico, but he is not part of that "fellahin" culture and its ahistorical stability is not afforded to him. His own modernity is inescapable, and his final part-ing from Dean returns to the wistful sense of loss and departure that is a recurring note: Sal watches as "Dean, ragged in a motheaten over-coat ... walked off alone, and the last I saw of him he rounded the corner of Seventh Avenue, eyes on the street ahead, and bent to it again" (309).

The final scene leaves Sal by the river, alone, as night falls on the world, an image echoing terms he used elsewhere: "So, as Spengler says, when comes the sunset of our culture ... lo, the clear, late-day glow reveals the original concerns again" ("Aftermath," 49). After countless predictions of final truth and understanding, reinventions of self, declarations of insight and revelation, the pearl is not what he expected. In the end, the only knowledge he claims is far more modest: "nobody, nobody knows what's going to happen to anybody besides the forlorn rags of growing old" (310). He is left, then, with the echo of another "forlorn man," ragged and old, the Ghost of the Susquehanna, who was last seen "dissolving in the darkness" (104–5). Dean, the man who guided him into all this, remains in his thoughts, along with Dean's ever-absent father, one of the ragged male figures whose full presence and knowledge is yearned for but never found. Kerouac took the line about God as Pooh Bear from Neal Cassady's children, and he inserts it here as a way of characterizing the naïveté of all our attempts at ultimate knowledge. The rags of Beat identity are all that Sal is left with as he sits by the river at nightfall contemplating the "raw land" and "all the people dreaming in the immensity of it" (309). The last paragraph combines thoughts of both beginnings and endings in its references to children and to "the coming of complete night." While the night "folds the final shore in," it too must be seen as part of the cyclical and creative movement of the myth of the rainy night, the endless and unmappable process of cultural history and personal identity that is Kerouac's road.

Notes and References

1. Historical Background

1. Jack Kerouac, "The Origins of the Beat Generation," in *Good Blonde and Others* (San Francisco: Grey Fox, 1993), 59; hereafter cited in the text as "Origins."

2. Jack Kerouac, "The Philosophy of the Beat Generation," in *Good Blonde and Others* (San Francisco: Grey Fox, 1993), 48.

3. Jack Kerouac, *Desolation Angels* (New York: Riverhead Books, 1995), 255–57.

2. The Importance of *On the Road*

1. William Burroughs, in Ann Charters, introduction to *On the Road*, by Jack Kerouac (New York: Penguin, 1991), xxviii.

2. Steven Watson, *The Birth of the Beat Generation: Visionaries, Rebels, and Hipsters, 1944–1960* (New York: Pantheon, 1995), 260.

3. Norman Podhoretz, "The Know-Nothing Bohemians," *Partisan Review* 25, no. 2 (Spring 1958): 311. Simon Frith, "The Cultural Study of Popular Music," in *Cultural Studies,* eds. Lawrence Grossberg, Cary Nelson, and Paula Treichler (New York: Routledge, 1992), 180.

4. Eldridge Cleaver, *Soul on Ice* (New York: Dell Ramparts, 1970), 74–77.

5. James Farrell, *The Spirit of the Sixties: The Making of Postwar Radicalism* (New York: Routledge, 1997), 66.

6. Dennis McNally, *Desolate Angel: Jack Kerouac, The Beat Generation, and America* (New York: Delta, 1979), 307; hereafter cited in the text.

7. Steve Turner, *Angelheaded Hipster: A Life of Jack Kerouac* (New York: Viking, 1996), 20.

8. Sven Birkerts, "On the Road to Nowhere: Kerouac Re-Read and Regretted," in *Contemporary Literary Criticism*, 61, ed. Roger Matuz (Detroit: Gale, 1990), 314; hereafter cited in the text.

9. Thomas Pynchon, *Slow Learner* (Boston: Little, Brown and Company, 1984), 7–9.

3. Critical Reception

1. Gilbert Millstein, "Books of the Time," *New York Times*, 5 September 1957, 27.

2. David Dempsey, "In Pursuit of Kicks," *New York Times*, 8 September 1957, 4.

3. Herbert Gold, "Hip, Cool, Beat—and Frantic," *The Nation*, 16 November 1957, 349.

4. Arthur Ossterreicher, "*On the Road*," *Village Voice*, 18 September 1957, 5.

5. John Clellon Holmes, quoted in Barry Gifford and Lawrence Lee, *Jack's Book: An Oral Biography of Jack Kerouac* (New York: St. Martin's Press, 1978), 240.

6. Barry Miles, *Jack Kerouac: King of the Beats* (London: Virgin, 1998), 263.

7. Carole Gottlieb Vopat, "Jack Kerouac's 'On the Road': A Re-Evaluation," in *Contemporary Literary Criticism*, 61, ed. Roger Matuz (Detroit: Gale, 1990), 303; hereafter cited in the text.

8. Melvin Askew, "Quests, Cars, and Kerouac," *University of Kansas Review* 28 (1962): 232.

9. Ellen G. Friedman, "Where Are the Missing Contents? (Post)Modernism, Gender, and the Canon." *PMLA* 108, no. 2 (1993): 249–50.

10. Dick Hebdige, *Subculture: The Meaning of Style* (London: Methuen, 1979), 47–48.

11. Tim Hunt, "The Misreading of Kerouac," *Review of Contemporary Fiction* 3, no. 2 (1983): 33.

12. Tim Hunt, *Kerouac's Crooked Road: The Development of a Fiction* (Berkeley: University of California Press, 1996), xxvi; hereafter cited in the text.

4. Setting Out

1. Gerald Nicosia, *Memory Babe: A Critical Biography of Jack Kerouac* (Berkeley: University of California Press, 1994), 343; hereafter cited in the text.

2. Leslie Fiedler, *Love and Death in the American Novel* (New York: Dell, 1966), 26; hereafter cited in the text.

3. Alan Nadel, *Containment Culture: American Narratives, Postmodernism, and the Atomic Age* (Durham: Duke University Press, 1995), 71.

4. John Clellon Holmes, *Nothing More to Declare* (New York: Dutton, 1967), 105.

5. Henry David Thoreau, *Walden and Resistance to Civil Government* (New York: Norton, 1992), 15; hereafter cited in the text.

6. Barbara Ehrenreich, *The Hearts of Men: American Dreams and the Flight from Commitment* (New York: Anchor Books, 1983), 12; hereafter cited in the text.

7. Joyce Johnson, introduction to *Desolation Angels,* by Jack Kerouac (New York: Riverhead Books, 1995), xiii.

8. Norman Mailer, "The White Negro," in *The Portable Beat Reader,* ed. Ann Charters (New York: Penguin, 1992), 585.

9. LeRoi Jones, *Blues People: Negro Music in White America* (New York: Morrow Quill Paperbacks, 1963), 181–82.

10. John Clellon Holmes, *Go* (New York: Thunder's Mouth Press, 1988), 36.

5. The First Journey

1. Jonathan Paul Eburne, "Trafficking in the Void: Burroughs, Kerouac, and the Consumption of Otherness," *Modern Fiction Studies* 42, no. 1 (Spring 1997): 54; hereafter cited in the text.

2. Allen Ginsberg, "Negative Capability: Kerouac's Buddhist Ethic," in *Disembodied Poetics: Annals of the Jack Kerouac School,* eds. Anne Waldman and Andrew Schelling (Albuquerque: University of New Mexico Press, 1994), 373.

3. Kerouac, "Aftermath: The Philosophy of the Beat Generation," in *Good Blonde & Others,* ed. Donald Allen (San Francisco: Grey Fox Press, 1993), 48.

4. Barry Gifford and Lawrence Lee, *Jack's Book: An Oral Biography of Jack Kerouac* (New York: St. Martin's Press, 1978), 232; hereafter cited in the text.

5. Tom Clarke, *Jack Kerouac: A Biography* (New York: Marlowe and Company, 1984), 168.

6. Oswald Spengler, *The Decline of the West,* 2 vols., trans. Charles Frances Atkinson (New York: Alfred A. Knopf, 1926), 169; hereafter cited in the text.

7. Allen Ginsberg, introduction to *Junkie,* by William Burroughs (New York: Penguin, 1977), vii.

8. Jack Kerouac, "On the Road Again," *New Yorker,* 22–29 June 1998, 48–50.

6. The Second Journey

1. Ross Russell, liner notes for Dexter Gordon and Wardell Gray, *The Hunt* (New York: Arista Records, 1977).

2. *A Jack Kerouac Romnibus,* produced and directed by Ralph Lombreglia and Kate Bernhardt (New York: Penguin, 1995).

3. Jack Kerouac, *Doctor Sax: Faust Part Three* (New York: Ballantine Books, 1973), 160.

4. Robert Creeley, citing Ed Dorn, "Thinking of Jack: A Preface," in *Good Blonde and Others,* by Jack Kerouac (San Francisco: Grey Fox, 1993), x.

7. The Third Journey

1. Thomas Pynchon, *Slow Learner* (Boston: Little, Brown and Company, 1984), 9.

2. Joyce Johnson, *Minor Characters: A Young Woman's Coming of Age in the Beat Orbit of Jack Kerouac* (New York: Anchor Books, 1994), xv.

8. The Final Journey

1. Edward Said, *Orientalism* (New York: Vintage, 1979), passim.

2. Jack Kerouac, *Visions of Cody* (New York: Penguin, 1993), 379.

Selected Bibliography

Primary Works

The Town and the City. New York: Harcourt, Brace and Company, 1950.

On the Road. New York: Viking Press, 1957.

The Subterraneans. New York: Grove Press, 1958.

The Dharma Bums. New York: Viking Press, 1958

Doctor Sax: Faust Part Three. New York: Grove Press, 1959.

Maggie Cassidy. New York: Avon Books, 1959.

Mexico City Blues. New York: Grove Press, 1959.

Visions of Cody. New York: New Directions, 1959.

The Scripture of the Golden Eternity. New York: Corinth Books, 1960.

Tristessa. New York: Avon Books, 1960.

Lonesome Traveler. New York: McGraw-Hill, 1960.

Book of Dreams. San Francisco: City Lights Books, 1961.

Pull My Daisy. New York: Grove Press, 1961.

Big Sur. New York: Farrar, Straus and Cudahy, 1962.

Visions of Gerard. New York: Farrar, Straus and Cudahy, 1963.

Desolation Angels. New York: Coward-McCann, 1965.

Satori in Paris. New York: Grove Press, 1966.

Vanity of Duluoz: An Adventurous Education, 1935–1946. New York: Coward-McCann, 1968.

Scattered Poems. San Francisco: City Lights Books, 1971.

Pic. New York: Grove Press, 1971.

Visions of Cody. New York: McGraw-Hill, 1972.

Heaven and Other Poems. San Francisco: Grey Fox, 1977.

Pomes All Sizes. San Francisco: City Lights Books, 1992.

Old Angel Midnight. San Francisco: Grey Fox, 1993.

Good Blonde and Others. San Francisco: Grey Fox, 1993.

Book of Blues. New York: Penguin, 1995.

Selected Letters, 1940–1956. Edited by Ann Charters. New York: Penguin, 1995.

Some of the Dharma. New York: Viking, 1997.

Secondary Works

Books

Cassady, Carolyn. *Off the Road: My Years with Cassady, Kerouac and Ginsberg.* New York: Penguin, 1990.

Charters, Ann. *Kerouac: A Biography.* New York: St. Martin's Press, 1994.

Clarke, Tom. *Jack Kerouac: A Biography.* New York: Marlowe and Company, 1984.

Donaldson, Scott, ed. *On the Road: Text and Criticism.* New York: Penguin Books, 1979.

Foster, Edward Halsey. *Understanding the Beats.* University of South Carolina Press, 1992.

French, Warren. *Jack Kerouac: Novelist of the Beat Generation.* Boston: Twayne, 1986.

Gifford, Barry, and Lawrence Lee. *Jack's Book: An Oral Biography of Jack Kerouac.* New York: St. Martin's Press, 1978.

Hipkiss, Robert A. *Jack Kerouac: Prophet of a New Romanticism.* Lawrence: Regents Press of Kansas, 1976.

Hunt, Tim. *Kerouac's Crooked Road: The Development of a Fiction.* Berkeley: University of California Press, 1996.

Johnson, Joyce. *Minor Characters: A Young Woman's Coming of Age in the Beat Orbit of Jack Kerouac.* New York: Anchor Books, 1994.

Lee, A. Robert, ed. *The Beat Generation Writers.* London: Pluto Press, 1996.

McNally, Dennis. *Desolate Angel: Jack Kerouac, The Beat Generation, and America.* New York: Delta, 1979.

Miles, Barry. *Jack Kerouac: King of the Beats.* London: Virgin, 1998.

Nicosia, Gerald. *Memory Babe: A Critical Biography of Jack Kerouac.* Berkeley: University of California Press, 1994.

Selected Bibliography

Stephenson, Gregory. *The Daybreak Boys: Essays on the Literature of the Beat Generation*. Carbondale: Southern Illinois University Press, 1990.

Turner, Steve. *Angelheaded Hipster: A Life of Jack Kerouac*. New York: Viking, 1996.

Tytell, John. *Naked Angels: Kerouac, Ginsberg, Burroughs*. New York: Grove Press, 1976.

Weinreich, Regina. *The Aesthetics of Spontaneity: A Study of the Fiction of Jack Kerouac*. Carbondale: Southern Illinois University Press, 1987.

Periodicals

Dharma Beat.

The Kerouac Connection.

The Kerouac Quarterly.

Moody Street Irregulars. 28 issues from Winter 1978 to Fall 1994.

Review of Contemporary Fiction 3, no. 2 (Summer 1983). Ed. John O'Brien.

Articles

Askew, Melvin W. "Quests, Cars, and Kerouac." *University of Kansas Review* 28 (1962): 231–40.

Blackburn, William. "Han Shan Gets Drunk with the Butchers: Kerouac's Buddhism in *On the Road,* The *Dharma Bums* and *Desolation Angels*." *Literature East and West* 21, nos. 1–4 (January–December 1977): 9–22.

Bowering, George. "*On The Road*: & the Indians at the End." *Stony Brook,* nos. 3/4 (1969): 191–201.

Dardess, George. "The Delicate Dynamics of Friendship: A Reconsideration of Jack Kerouac's *On the Road*." *American Literature* 46 (May 1974): 200–206.

———. "Jack Kerouac As Religious Teacher." *Moody Street Irregulars: A Jack Kerouac Newsletter,* no. 1 (1978): 4–6.

———. "The Logic of Spontaneity: A Reconsideration of Kerouac's 'Spontaneous Prose Method.' " *Boundary 2,* no. 3 (1975): 729–43.

D'Orso, Michael. "Man Out of Time: Kerouac, Spengler, and the 'Faustian Soul.' " *Studies in American Fiction* 11, no. 1 (Spring 1983): 19–30.

Ellis, R. J. " 'I'm Only a Jolly Storyteller': Jack Kerouac's *On the Road* and *Visions of Cody*." In *The Beat Generation Writers,* edited by A. Robert Lee. London: Pluto Press, 1996.

Ginsberg, Allen. "Negative Capability: Kerouac's Buddhist Ethic." In *Disembodied Poetics: Annals of the Jack Kerouac School,* edited by Anne Waldman and Andrew Schelling. Albuquerque: University of New Mexico Press, 1994.

Gussow, Adam. "Bohemia Revisited: Malcolm Cowley, Jack Kerouac and *On the Road*." *Georgia Review* 38, no. 2 (Summer 1984): 291–311.

Holton, Robert. "Kerouac among the Felaheen: *On the Road* to the Postmodern." *Modern Fiction Studies* 41, no. 2 (Summer 1995): 265–83.

Vopat, Carole Gottlieb. "Jack Kerouac's *On the Road*: A Re-Evaluation." *Midwest Quarterly* 14 (1973): 385–407.

There are a number of Internet sites devoted to Kerouac and the Beats that contain useful material as well as aids to further exploration. A good starting place is "Literary Kicks," a site maintained by Levi Asher (http://www.charm.net/~brooklyn/).

Index

African American culture, 51–52,
69–70, 89–92, 101, 117;
admiration for, 70, 83, 92, 98-
99; "happy Negro," 9, 92, 98-
99. *See also* fellahin
Askew, Melvin, 13
Auschwitz, 35
Autry, Gene, 21, 64

Beat Generation, The, 8
beatniks, 8, 100 (*see also* hip culture)
bebop, 10, 35–36, 68–69
Beyond Conformity (Winston
White), 5
Birkerts, Sven, 9, 10
bohemians, 8
Brando, Marlon, 7, 12, 84
Burroughs, Joan Vollmer Adams, 78
Burroughs, William, 8, 57, 78, 79,
107; *Naked Lunch*, 19

Capote, Truman, 12
Cassady, Carolyn, 103

Cassady, Neal, 29, 79, 83, 99, 124;
letters to, 48, 53, 54, 55-56
Chaplin, Charlie, 64
Civil Rights Movement, 62,70, 90
Clarke, Tom, 57
Cleaver, Eldridge: *Soul on Ice*, 9
Cold War, 5, 8, 21, 42
conformism, 5, 8, 56, 94, 106
Conrad, Joseph: *Heart of Darkness*,
43–44, 119
Cooper, James Fenimore, 28
Coward, Noel, 47
Creeley, Robert, 87
Cru, Henri, 31, 52, 53, 54

Dardess, George, 13
Dean, James, 7, 84
Deleuze, Gilles and Felix Guattari:
Anti-Oedipus, 15
Dempsey, David, 12
Denver, Bob, 8
Dostoyevsky, Fyodor, 48, 49, 68, 84;
The Possessed, 84

Dylan, Bob, 9

Easy Rider, 84
Eburne, Jonathan Paul, 40, 54
Ehrenreich, Barbara, 26, 74

Ellison, Ralph, 91
Esquire, 7

Federal-Aid Highway Act, 4
fellahin, 83, 91; Dean and, 71, 77;
    derivation of, 57–58; and jazz,
    100, 102; Sal and, 60, 61, 62,
    63, 72, 90, 112, 116–23
Fiedler, Leslie, 19, 28, 34
Fitzgerald, F. Scott: The Great
    Gatsby, 19
Foucault, Michel, 76
Franco, Bea, 57, 58
Freud, Sigmund, 26
Friedman, Ellen 14
Frith, Simon, 9, 63

G.I. Bill, 4
Gaillard, Slim, 88
gender, 24–29, 52, 71–74, 85–86,
    94–95, 96–98, 101–3
"Get Your Kicks on Route 66," 4
Ghost of the Susquehanna, 65, 124
Gibson, Harry "The Hipster," 88
Gifford, Barry and Lawrence Lee, 57
Gillespie, Dizzy, 35, 88
Gilligan's Island, 8
Ginsberg, Allen, 9, 29, 48, 63, 78,
    82; "Howl," 19, 36, 46, 102;
    letter to 54, 55, 106–7
Goethe, Johann Wolfgang: The Sor-
    rows of Young Werther, 30
Gold, Herbert, 12
Gone with the Wind, 61
Gordon, Dexter and Wardell Gray:
    The Hunt, 68–69, 72
Growing Up Absurd (Paul Good-
    man), 5

Harper's, 10
Hayden, Tom, 9
Hebdige, Dick, 14
Hemingway, Ernest, 46, 64
Himes, Chester, 91
Hinkle, Al, 102
Hinkle, Helen, 102–3
hip culture, 35–37, 48, 78, 84, 93,
    102, 120–21
Hiroshima, 35
Holmes, John Clellon, 21, 47; Go,
    36; "This Is the Beat Genera-
    tion," 11, 12
Hollywood, 8, 42, 47, 63–64, 87,
    109–10; movie imagery, 61,
    63–64, 109; and movie ver-
    sion, 10, 84
Hombre, 42
homosexuality, 55–56
Hoover, J. Edgar, 8

How To Win Friends and Influence
    People (Dale Carnegie), 4
"Howl," 7 (see also Ginsberg, Allen)
Hunt, Tim, 13, 15, 34, 45
Huxley, Aldous: Brave New World, 5

identity: Beat identity, 48, 54,
    109–11; instability and imper-
    manence of, 40, 48, 62–64,
    86–87, 88, 123–24; of post-
    war American youth, 30; Sal's
    identity crises, 40–41, 54–55,
    63–65

jazz, 6, 88, 91–92, 98–101, 117 (see
    also bebop)
Johnson, Joyce, 31; Minor Charac-
    ters, 102–3
Jones, LeRoi (Amiri Baraka), 36

Kafka, Franz, 81
Kerouac, Jack, first-person narrative,
    19–20; maps, 31–32, 33, 41,

45; myth of the rainy night, 33, 38, 77, 79–81, 82, 86–87, 88, 94, 104, 106, 122, 124; publication of *On the Road*, 3, 7–8, 10, 11–12; spontaneous prose, 10

CHARACTERS IN *ON THE ROAD*

Camille (Carolyn Cassady), 58, 66, 72, 73; marriage to Dean, 67, 94–95, 102, 123

Carlo Marx (Allen Ginsberg), 71, 84; and alternative subculture, 29, 47– 49; and the "last thing," 49, 75

Chad King (Hal Chase), 42, 46, 120

Dean Moriarty (Neal Cassady), 21–29, 30, 46, 47, 71–72, 74–77, 80, 82–84, 85–86, 94–98, 99, 102, 107, 110, 111, 112–16, 117, 118–19, 121, 122,123; and African American culture, 69–70, 71, 77, 79, 88, 101; as cowboy, 21–22, 27, 42; as hipster, 48, 93; and "IT," 75, 103–4, 113; madness of, 24–25, 28, 67–68, 85, 95, 105, 106, 108–9, 123; marriage of, 67, 87, 94–95, 123; sexuality of, 23, 25–26, 49, 74, 83–84, 97

Eddie, 40–41, 53

Ed Dunkel (Al Hinkle) 29, 67, 73, 97, 102

Ed Wall (Don Uhl), 82

Elmer Hassel (Herbert Hinkle), 29, 84

Frankie, 105–06

Galatea Dunkel (Helen Hinkle), 73, 95, 97, 98, 115; marriage to Ed, 67, 68, 73, 102

Ghost of the Susquehanna, 65, 124

Hal Hingham (Alan Harrington), 82

Hyman Solomon, 77

Inez, 58

Jane Lee (Joan Vollmer Adams Burroughs), 29, 78

Lee Ann, 52, 96

Lucille, 73

Marylou (Luanne Henderson), 26, 49, 52, 67, 84, 88, 93, 94; and cowboy image, 27, 64; and Sal, 58, 58, 74, 85; as whore, 27, 72, 86

Mississippi Gene, 43–44, 47

Old Bull Lee (William S. Burroughs), 29, 73, 78–79, 81, 84

Remi Boncoeur (Henri Cru), 31, 51–53

Rita Bettencourt, 50, 58, 107

Roland Major (Allen Temko), 46–47, 49, 64

Rollo Greb (Alan Ansen), 75

Roy Johnson (Bill Tomson), 29, 95, 96

Stan Shephard (Frank Jeffries), 114, 115

Terry (Bea Franco), 61, 64, 73, 85; as Chicana, 56, 59–60, 106; and fellahin, 57, 59, 60, 61, 62, 63, 72, 90

Tim Gray (Ed White), 114

Tommy Snark (Jim Holmes), 29

Walter, 101–02

WORKS

"Aftermath: The Philosophy of the Beat Generation," 58, 123

Desolation Angels, 6

Dharma Bums, 108

Doctor Sax, 79, 81

Letters, 20, 21, 32, 51, 52, 108, 110, 120; to Ginsberg, 46, 79 (*see also* Ginsberg, Allen). *See also* Cassady, Neal

"On the Road Again," 70

"Origins of the Beat Generation, The," 6, 32, 101

Visions of Cody, 120, 121

Kerouac, Joan Haverty (wife), 19
Kerouac, Leo (father), 20
Kesey, Ken, 99
Krebs, Maynard G., 8

Lake, Veronica, 64
Lennon, John, 9
Life, 7
London, Jack, 64

Mad, 8
Mademoiselle, 7
Mailer, Norman: "The White
    Negro," 35, 44, 56, 69, 98
Man in the Grey Flannel Suit, The
    (Sloan Wilson), 5
Mansfield, Jayne, 26
Many Loves of Dobie Gillis, The, 8
Mark of Zorro, The, 64
Marx, Groucho, 95
McCarthyism, 5
McCrea, Joel, 64
Melville, Herman, 28, 31; *Moby
    Dick*, 19, 34, 108–9
Meredith, Burgess, 64
Midnight Cowboy, 42
Misfits, The, 42
Millstein, Gilbert, 7, 11
modernity: and alienation of spirit,
    56, 62, 80–81, 90–91; and
    fellahin, 83, 90–90, 112,
    116–117, 119–23; and its
    rejection/transcendence, 71,
    88, 99, 108, 112; and those
    excluded, 6, 62, 70, 83, 90–91
Modigliani, Amedeo, 26

Monk, Thelonious, 35
Monroe, Marilyn, 26

Nadel, Alan, 21
Nation, The, 12

Native American culture, 40, 45 (*see
    also* fellahin)
Newman, Paul, 42
New York Times, 7, 11, 12
Nicosia, Gerald, 45, 57, 58–59, 78,
    84
Nietzsche, Friedrich, 25, 71

Of Mice and Men, 64
Organization Man, The (William H.
    Whyte), 5
Orwell, George: *1984*, 5

Parker, Charlie, 35, 88
Parker, Edie, 20, 52
passing, 90
pastoralism, 61–62, 92
Petry, Ann, 91
Playboy, 7
Podhoretz, Norman, 9, 63,70
police: and "cop-souls," 5, 34–35,
    59, 75–77, 114–15; Sal/Ker-
    ouac's police work, 52–54
postmodernism, 71
Power of Positive Thinking, The
    (Norman Vincent Peale), 4
Prescott, Orville, 11
Presley, Elvis, 84
Proust, Marcel: *Remembrance of
    Things Past (A la Recherche du
    Temps Perdu)*, 83
Pynchon, Thomas: *Slow Learner*,
    9–10, 99

Rabelais, Francois, 52, 113
race, 9, 62, 69–70, 89–93, 117
Reich, Wilhelm, 26, 100
Rexroth, Kenneth, 91
Riesman, David: *The Lonely Crowd*,
    5
Rimbaud, Arthur, 49
Roach, Max, 10
Rosenberg, Julius and Ethel, 5
Route 66, 4

Index

Russell, Ross, 68–69

Said, Edward: *Orientalism*, 119
Salinger, J. D.: *The Catcher in the Rye*, 19

Sampas, Sebastian, 57
Saroyan, William, 64
Shakespeare, William: "Sonnet 30," 83
Spengler, Oswald: and fellahin, 57–58, 117–18, 121; *The Decline of the West*, 57, 113, 121; theory of rise and fall of empires, 57–58, 81, 88, 117–18, 123
Steinbeck, John: *The Grapes of Wrath*, 4, 106
Stewart, Slam, 88

Sullivan's Travels, 64

Thoreau, Henry David, 106–7, 108; *Walden*, 24, 32, 34, 35,
totalitarianism, 56
Twain, Mark, 28; *The Adventures of Huckleberry Finn*, 19, 22, 24, 38, 93
Tytell, John, 13

Village Voice, 12
Vopat, Carole, 13

Weinreich, Regina, 13
Whitman, Walt, 21, 31, 34; "Song of the Open Road," 31
Wild One, The, 84
Wright, Richard, 91; *Native Son*, 35

About the Author

Robert Holton teaches at Okanagan University College (Kelowna, B.C., Canada), where he specializes in American literature and critical theory. A graduate of University of London (M.A.) and McGill University (Ph.D.), he is the author of *Jarring Witnesses: Modern Fiction and the Representation of History* (1995), as well as numerous articles on American literature and critical theory.

The Editor

Robert Lecker is professor of English at McGill University in Montreal. He received his Ph.D. from York University. Lecker is the author of numerous critical studies, including *On the Line* (1982), *Robert Kroetch* (1986), *An Other I* (1988), and *Making It Real: The Canonization of English-Canadian Literature* (1995). He is the editor of the critical journal *Essays on Canadian Writing* and of many collections of critical essays, the most recent of which is *Canadian Canons: Essays in Literary Value* (1991). He is the founding and current general editor of Twayne's Masterwork Studies and the editor of the Twayne World Authors Series on Canadian writers. He is also the general editor of G. K. Hall's Critical Essays on World Literature series.